THOUGHTS ON THINGS FINANCIAL

Beaux Remy Press

Beaux Remy Press
2212 Canterbury Drive,
Mansfield, Texas 76063

ISBN: 978-1-7348490-0-4 (print)
ISBN: 978-1-7348490-1-1(ebook)

Ordering Information:
Special discounts are available on quantity purchases by corporations, associa-
tions, and others. For details, contact:
Shelly Schulz

817-271-4602

shelly.schulz@schulzwealth.com

1752 Broad Park Circle North, Suite 110,

Mansfield, TX 76063

TABLE OF CONTENTS

THOUGHTS ON THINGS FINANCIAL

YOUR GUIDE TO A CHAOTIC MONEY WORLD

ROBERT R. SCHULZ, CFP ®

Chapter 1

PLANNING IS IMPORTANT... THAT IS, IF YOU EVER REALLY WANT TO GET ANYWHERE

"Do you want to know?" I asked the question honestly and sincerely and waited for a reply. The man in front of me looked nervous. We were sitting in a spare office near the break room, surrounded by offcast computer and phone equipment. I was sitting precariously on a wobbly chair that obviously nobody else wanted either. Any way you looked at it, this was an inhospitable and uncomfortable environment.

I was tired. My plane from DFW to Milwaukee had been delayed the night before. I had brushed away the light layer of snow from the windshield of my rental car at 5:00 a.m. to be in Fond du Lac by 7:00 that morning, and then I had driven three and a half hours to be in Eau Claire by late afternoon.

It felt a little odd for me to be sitting there in a spare office on the south bank of Lake Winnebago in chilly December. "I'm getting too old for this," I thought to myself. Back home in Texas, I had a thriving financial planning practice. At age 50, with a quarter of a century of experience under my belt, I didn't need to be out on the road like this. Yet there I was because deep down in my soul

I knew I wanted to be there, at the transformative intersection of life and planning. That was my calling.

In that brief moment, as I waited for a response from the anxious man across from me, I wondered how many times I had asked that question. It was a follow-up question to one I had asked just a few times more over the course of my career: "Do you know what it's going to take for you to retire someday?"

"Not really." "No." "I've never really thought about it." "I have no idea." Those were the answers I usually received. We all start our careers with forty years or so between where we are and retirement, but over time that space diminishes. Then, suddenly, we look up and realize that crucial time is quickly passing. One of my jobs as a financial planner is to be a catalyst for that realization. So, you'll find me wherever there are people who want to know what retirement requires.

For me, the road to that day in Eau Claire had started 30 years earlier in Charleston, South Carolina, where I had served as a young naval officer aboard a destroyer, the USS John Rodgers. I learned quickly upon reporting for duty that many of the young sailors in my division aboard ship were barely subsisting on low wages and had very little financial knowledge. They were prime targets for financial scams and usury. I spent a lot of my time helping these sailors and their families with budgeting, debt, and cash management. I even put myself through the Volunteer Income Tax Assistance (VITA) program so that I could help the 300 souls on my ship file their tax returns for free. This kept them clear of the predatory practices of tax refund loan advance scams that were so prevalent off base.

When I resigned my commission in the Navy, I knew I wanted to be a financial planner, but I didn't know how or what to do in order to become one. Naively, I ended up accepting a job as a life insurance agent and registered representative with a large, well-respected financial services company. It was a 100% commission sales position. I worked relentlessly hard but barely struggled to make a living in the first year. In my second year, I found myself making a very good living, but the more I learned about the products I was selling, the less enthusiastic I became about selling them. Soon I was standing at a very difficult crossroads: I was going to have to decide whether I wanted to keep selling products for my employer or provide sound financial advice for my clients. Clearly, to me, the two were mutually exclusive. That's when I started to move on toward, eventually, over time, creating my own wealth management practice.

It's been a long road, but today my practice is fully dedicated to providing comprehensive financial planning and investment solutions in a way that directly benefits my clients, not the financial services industry that most advisors are required to serve. Now, with all of the knowledge and experience I have garnered over the years, there are some important concepts I want to convey. This book is my attempt to help as many people as possible avoid all of the traps and pitfalls out there and achieve financial success.

"Yes," he said. "I want to know what it's going to take to retire someday." An uncomfortable pause followed as I snapped out of my daydream and became mentally present again. My lack of sleep and weariness from the long drive was starting to catch up with me. "Okay," I said. We started running through some numbers and calculations. It didn't take long. Every time I run a quick retirement readiness scenario, it's the same in many ways but always a little different for each person's situation. In this man's case, he had some things working in his favor. The owner of his company, my client, was very benevolent, cared deeply about his employees' wellbeing, and believed fervently in the retirement plan I managed for them. This employee was contributing 3% of his pay into the retirement plan. It was being matched with another 3%, and yet another 3% was contributed to his account as an annual, end-of-year profit-sharing contribution. That's 9% of his total pay that was getting invested for his benefit.

The surprising thing was that he didn't even know that his employer was contributing twice as much to his retirement as he was. Because of this, with a few adjustments, his retirement scenario worked out pretty well, and for the first time in his life, he knew that. That's a big deal, to know, and yet most people don't know.

Neither he nor hardly any others I've met with ever thought about retirement in terms of a financial plan until I showed up. Based upon my experiences, I have to assume most Americans have never actually planned for retirement. I'm not passing judgement here, just stating an observation. A quick Google search provides some staggering statistics about how low the average savings rate for retirement is in the U.S., but very little, too little, is written or discussed about the need for a plan.

Many of us work so hard to be successful in our professional lives only to leave our personal financial success completely to fate, just hoping it will all work out on its own. I see it frequently. Many times, I'll ask people, "How did you come up with the deferral you are making in your 401(k) towards retirement?" An overwhelming majority of the time, their answer has to do with how much match they are receiving from their employer, or it's the default that was setup when they were hired, or it's how much they think they can afford. Very rarely does anybody ever tell me, "I came up with that number based upon how much money I will need to retire." That's the right answer, every time, because it's based upon a plan for future personal financial success.

For the vast majority of us, it will be to our detriment to ignore the planning required for what we need. Sure, there are people out there who will attain personal financial success without planning, but they are outliers. They take extreme risk, get very lucky, and are somehow able to avoid the issue altogether. Good for them.

But there is no need to take extreme risk or leave our personal financial success up to luck if we plan.

There is an entire industry of get rich quick schemes out there, preying on those who are desperate to find an easy way to succeed financially in their personal lives. Maybe you enjoy spending large sums of money on seminars about real estate and options investing or get a big kick out of persuading your friends and family to buy and market products and services through multi-level marketing. If that's you, then fine, but you don't need to do this. All you really need is a financial plan.

But most American's won't take the time to sit down, focus, and decide what it is they want to achieve from a personal financial standpoint. There are lots of good excuses for putting this off: It's complicated. It's hard to find someone you can trust to help. And it's hard to find the time in our busy work and family lives. If you don't think you have time, then you're right, you *are* running out of time. You'll have to make time because we all lose a little more of this precious resource every day, and time is a critical component in the time value of money concept we will discuss later as the lynchpin to your personal financial success.

Along the way you will find that there are a lot of advisors and companies out there who are not worthy of your trust. In this book, I'll teach you how to distinguish those who can truly help you from those who are just wanting to sell you their expensive products. As life happens, there are a multitude of things that pull at our financial resources. Sometimes it's hard to know what to do. I'll help you frame and prioritize your goals so you can make good decisions. You will also learn how to expect the unexpected, and I'll help you be better prepared for some of the bad things that you and your family may have to deal with. Also, in our quest for financial success, we can sometimes be our own worst enemy. There are tricks and systems I can teach you that will help you manage savings and debt in a way that enhances rather than detracts from your long-term goals.

This book is designed to provide a guide, in basic English without all of the fancy financial terms, with the right information you need to step up to the plate with confidence. With the basic knowledge I'll provide, once you step up it should not be that hard from there. But stepping up *is* hard. For over 25 years, I've been working with people just like you to help them achieve personal financial success. By far the greatest trap is not ever starting and, therefore, never having a plan until it's too late.

Time and again, couples, when they set an appointment for an initial visit, will say things like, "We've been planning on coming to see you for years." To which I always reply, "Why did you wait so long?" Generally, their replies will revolve around getting debt paid off, or they wanted to get some 401(k) contributions going, or maybe they wanted to finish up paying for their kid's college. All important goals, but why did these things keep them from starting their plan? Maybe they incorrectly thought that these were mutually exclusive goals. In reality, though, anything having to do with your personal finances has everything to do with your long-term financial success.

Trying to plan for retirement in a vacuum is rarely going to work out. All of these other financial goals are important too, and most importantly, they are interrelated. Why? Mainly due to time. We have some variables we can control when planning for personal financial success, but there are others we cannot control. Of those factors we cannot control, time is the biggest.

When a new client comes in for the first time and says they have been meaning to come see me for years, my heart sinks deep down into my stomach because I know we will not get those years back. We won't have the time we would have had otherwise and making up for lost time is the hardest planning to accomplish. We can make up for down markets in recessions as long as we have time. We can make up for not having enough money to set aside as long as we have time for the funds to compound. The less time we have, the harder it gets to accomplish personal financial success.

So, whenever people ask me when the right time is to get started with a financial plan, I always say, "Right now." Don't wait another minute because every single day counts when it comes to compounding interest. You think you're too young? Maybe you're not even sure what you want yet from a personal financial success standpoint. It doesn't matter. Get started now. Get the ship pointed in the right direction; otherwise, you may at some point find yourself halfway to nowhere, lost at sea without a plan and with limited resources.

Unfortunately, many Americans *are* lost at sea when it comes to their personal finances. But I can tell you from experience, there are plenty of people on track with a plan, saving, living financially stable lives, providing adequately for their family, and securing their future. You don't have to be a millionaire to have a financial plan. But having a financial plan might make you a millionaire. All you have to do is start *now*.

Chapter 2

THE GREATEST STORY EVER TOLD (ABOUT MONEY)

I think I was around 10 years old when my dad first talked to me about the magic of compounding interest. It really stuck with me, and its impact on me was a big reason why I became a financial advisor and planner. My dad had been a stockbroker with Smith Barney in the 60s and early 70s. By this time, he had moved on and was working for my granddad in the family newspaper business. Individual Retirement Accounts, or IRAs, had just come into existence, and he wanted me to open one for myself, at 10! I think the conversation started with that classic 10-year-old question, "Are we rich?" To which my dad had responded with the classic response, "Yes, we're rich because we have all that we need, and we have each other." That didn't cut it for me, so from there I asked, "So we are millionaires?"

Dad deftly dodged a direct response and said, "You know, son, if you want to be a millionaire, it's easily within your reach. If you took $2,000 per year and invested it at a 6% return, by the time you were 65, you would have a million dollars." "No way!" I said. He walked me through it on his old TI-30 calculator, where he had me take the initial $2,000 and multiply it by 1.06, then multiply the result again by the same number 55 times. That's how I learned about compounding. Later I would learn that the equation we ran is exponential, and, on a graph, it's not a straight line. Rather, it arcs or curves upward. The graph starts out with little curve to it. Then, as the asset value grows, the curve steepens.

Over years working with families as they save for retirement, I've learned that saving the first chunk of money is the tricky part. *Any* amount of money saved initially is crucial. Why? Because the magic of compounding has to start somewhere, or it doesn't start at all. If it starts with $2,000 at age 10, we are well on our way. But let's be real. Life is not a straight line where everything just works out nice and orderly. Dealing with the challenges of building a career and raising a family, along with the setbacks that are a part of everyone's life experience, makes saving for retirement difficult, especially early on where it's most important. We stop saving when we have kids because of the cost of daycare or the financial strain of going down to a single income. We stop saving when we bite off that big mortgage for a new home. We spend money from our 401(k) to relocate for new jobs.

For whatever reason, we tend to think of life as linear, graphically illustrated as a straight line. From a linear standpoint, these are not bad decisions. We think we can make it up by taking care of what needs to be done now and then buckling down later to get our long-term retirement savings handled. When we put off investing money toward our future, we don't get that time back. That's what my dad was trying to convey to me 40 years ago and something I passionately know that I want to convey to anyone who will listen. When you get to a certain age (and it's a different age for different people), you finally start to *really* understand this finite time issue and how difficult it is to make up for lost time.

For instance, let's say I blew my dad off at age 10 and waited until I was out of college and in the Navy before starting to save. Twelve years multiplied by $2,000 means I'm just $24k behind, right?

On a linear line, I'd be just $24K short of a million at retirement. That's no big deal. But that's not how it actually works. Run the numbers on a calculator the way my dad and I did, and you'll find I'm around a *half a million short*. That measly $2,000 per year on the front end, compounded, eventually represented 50% of what I could have accumulated.

In another scenario, let's say that at age 35 I decide to take the $50,000 or so that has accumulated in my IRA and pay off consumer debt and a home equity loan that has become a nagging nuisance. From a linear standpoint it makes sense. I'll be able to free up some cash flow and eliminate the interest payments. Well, it better free up some serious *cha-ching* because, if we run the numbers, instead of continuing with my $2,000 per year contributions, I must now save around $12,000 per year to hit $1 million at age 65. I now must save *six times as much money* in order to hit my initial goal.

With the right information, we can see that this is a terrible idea. I should, at a minimum, preserve my retirement savings. Don't forget that it's in an account designed for retirement, an IRA. IRAs are cool because they allow us to defer taxes on the contributions and gains until we start using the money, but if we tap the account early, prior to age 59 and a half, the IRS charges us a 10% tax penalty on the withdrawal. So, in order to use it at age 35, I have to pay taxes and a 10% penalty on the entire withdrawal. Conservatively, that may leave me with only $35,000 of the $50,000 IRA balance to use toward paying off debt. Definitely not worth it. In compounding language, that $50,000 may be the equivalent of $300,000 at age 65 and, therefore, represents 30% of my $1 million goal. There's no way I would throw away 30% of my retirement goal at age 35. That's ridiculous!

You see, it's much easier to make good financial decisions when we understand the power of compounding. Let's look at that last scenario from a positive, long-term perspective. *Because* my 10-year-old self saved $2,000 per year, I had $50,000 in my IRA by the time I was 35. It may not sound like a lot of money to you, but that $50,000 represents $10,000 a year in free cash flow that I would not have otherwise. How? Because, if I waited until age 35 to start saving, it would take $12,000 per year instead of $2,000 per year of savings to reach my goal. I should use that free cash flow to accelerate a debt paydown strategy, move on, and try not to do that to myself again. Then, over time, over my working life, my retirement savings will continue to free up cash flow. Why? Because as my IRA grows, the compounding does the saving for me.

What a deal! If we start saving as early as possible for retirement, the compounding of our investment will free up cash flow for us to use in other areas of our life. By "as early as possible," I mean right now. If you're a little older than 10, that's okay; it still works. But I'm certainly not a spring chicken at this point. You may not be either, so what do we do with the time we have?

You know, I have a lot of clients who get caught up in that really heavy, expensive part of life when you're raising kids, trying to educate them, and get them out on their own. Understandably, retirement savings sometimes get put on the back burner during this period of time. Hey, you know what? Maybe there's just not anything you can do about that. But the good news is, if you can come out of this expensive period of life unscathed (without significant debt or a massive hemorrhaging of your retirement savings), then there is hope. Your expenses are less now, and you are probably on top of your game professionally and enjoying the highest earnings of your career.

I have a client couple just like this, and they were making up for lost time with sheer, brute force saving. The hard part for them was getting their arms around this massive shift in the redeployment of their resources. To get our arms around it, we had to calculate it.

When they first came to me, they had no idea where to start, what was feasible, or even what they wanted to accomplish. We started at ground zero and created a clear snapshot of their financial situation: how much they make, how much they spend, the value of all of their assets and any liabilities. There was definitely some good news. They had zero debt and had even paid off their mortgage. They had more than adequate cash reserves too. This was because they were both making a lot of money. Their careers took off at about the same time that their two kids launched. They suddenly had $30K less in expenses (last year of college) and almost $45K more in income. This sudden change in their cash flow allowed them to pay off some nagging debt and their mortgage, increase their 401(k) deferrals to maximum levels (around $48K total), and put another $5,000 per month in additional savings. We had a good laugh thinking about how their younger selves could not have imagined savings numbers this big. But this is what late-stage retirement planning is about: power.

From ground zero, we moved to D-Day: the date they wanted to shoot for as their jumping-off point. Instinctively, they knew their late-stage plan would need as much runway as possible and chose age 70 (17 years out) for their target retirement date. We talked about what they thought retirement was going to look like, what they wanted to do, and how their expenses would change. A key discovery here was that one spouse was thinking more of a working retirement. He had achieved a level of experience and expertise in his career he believed could demand decent part time consulting income. It would require some travel, but they were both excited about the prospect of travelling together for his consulting engagements.

After identifying their current situation, discussing their plans and dreams for the future, and calculating the retirement scenarios, I'm happy to say we were able to come up with a retirement plan they were both very excited about. That was several years ago. In our most recent semi-annual meeting, they were actually ahead of the game and saving much more money than we originally planned for or even thought possible.

More on Rate of Return

Hopefully these examples have helped you better understand the importance of starting your retirement saving as soon as possible. Maintaining a consistent savings strategy is hard but maintaining a consistent investing strategy can be even more difficult. A majority of us in the workforce are relying heavily on 401(k) plans and IRAs to fund our retirement. These plans and accounts require us to choose suitable investments, usually with very little assistance or support. That's a lot of pressure.

In my example where my dad showed me the way to riches, I used an assumed rate of return of 6%. Why? How did I come up with that? The answer may surprise you. Believe it or not, I remember that day so well, that I remember my dad using 6%. He came up with 6% because, back then, Bank CDs, or Certificates of Deposit, were paying 6% interest, and that's what most people used as an investment vehicle in their IRAs. This was before the proliferation of mutual funds and the discount brokerages that make it so much easier now to invest effectively, so most people just put their retirement savings on deposit at their local bank. That's what a CD is. My how times have changed. By the time I started my advisory career in 1994, 6% CD yields were a thing of the past.

My dad got that part wrong, but we'll forgive him because *most* people forget a very, very important factor in our retirement equation that eliminates CDs as an investment option: inflation. Every year, things get more expensive, and we call this inflation. Inflation is a slow erosion of purchasing power over time. It's hard to see, just like it's hard to tell a flower bud is blooming if you simply stare at it. But when you come back the next day, you clearly see the change. The US Government measures this erosion of purchasing power, and they call it the Consumer Price Index. They have a cool calculator on their website, where you can plug in past years and see how much inflation has eroded the purchasing power of your money: https://data.bls.gov/cgi-bin/cpicalc.pl. And here a chart from Investopedia shows the buying power of $100 eroding over time, going all the way back to 1799!

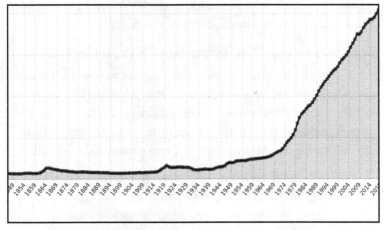

https://www.investopedia.com/ask/answers/042415/what-impact-does-infla-tion-have-time-value-money.asp

If I input the period of time from when I was 10 years old to now in the inflation calculator, it says it will take over $4 million today to buy what $1 million would buy back then. Dang! I was shooting for the wrong number. The moral of the story here is we have to assume there will be inflation and account for it as we plan for retirement.

This brings up another important point we need to understand. Let's say my dad answered my question, "Are we millionaires?" with, "Yes, son, and, by the way, here's a million bucks." Now, let's assume I buried it in the backyard in a time capsule, only to be opened in 2020. I open the time capsule, and, amazingly, it's all there. I didn't lose any of it. Or did I? It's really only worth about a quarter of what it was, so on a *real return* basis, I lost 75% of it by burying it in the backyard for 42 years.

But I don't think my dad would have let me do that. Instead, let's say I invested in CDs. If I had invested my million dollars in CDs, I *might* have barely kept up with inflation. In order for the compounding magic to work, we have to make a real return over and above the inflation rate. Later in the book, we'll get into how to build an investment portfolio to beat inflation.

TAX DEFERRALS: THE GIFT THAT KEEPS ON GIVING

In order to get the magic of the time value of money really humming along, we also have to take taxes into account. Just about every time we make money in the United States of America, we have to pay taxes on it. This includes investment returns, such as capital gains and interest, not just what you make from your day job.

The government incentivizes us to save and spend our money in certain ways. We get tax deductions for things like charitable contributions and property taxes because the government wants to encourage us to give money to charity and own our own homes. We are also encouraged to invest in specially designated accounts that provide tax incentives for retirement savings. The most common tax incentive for retirement savings is found in 401(k)s and IRAs, and we call it tax-deferred savings. "Tax deferred" means you don't pay taxes on the front end. Instead, the government allows you to pay it later, as you distribute the money to yourself in retirement. This means the money we put into our IRA or 401(k) is not considered income for tax purposes in the year we contribute, and it means all of the investment return we make is not taxed until later.

In other words, you get to make money on the money that the IRS let you keep. This is a big deal. Why? Because it allows the magic of the time value of money to become even more magical. It steepens the curve of compounding significantly, since the tax burden is deferred. Let's say your brother-in-law, who lives in California, owns a parcel of property in East Texas. You make a deal with him. If he allows you to harvest the timber on his land for 30 years, you'll keep track of the timber income and pay him at the end of the 30-year term. If he agrees, he is allowing you to invest the harvest income and keep whatever return you are able to make on what is really his money. That's a good deal for you and similar to what the government allows in tax-deferred accounts.

But since the dawning of the IRA and 401(K), the government has established another tax incentive for saving for retirement, and that's the Roth IRA. When you invest money in a Roth, you pay your taxes up front. Any money you put into a Roth is taxed in the year you contribute to it. But once invested, it grows tax free, never to be molested by the government again. In magical time value of money terms, this puts us squarely in fairy tale territory. Granted, we start with money that was already taxed, but over time, we get steep compounding of money with no tax load on the return. Then, when we get to retirement, we can pull it out of the account and use the money without paying any additional taxes. Just like any of this tax related stuff, there is complexity around income limits on contributions, Roth IRAs, Roth 401(k)s, conversion strategies, backdoor Roth strategies, and more.

If your modified adjusted gross income for income tax purposes is below the limit ($196,000 for married and filing jointly in 2020), you are probably eligible to make contributions to a Roth IRA, and you should probably take advantage of this. If your income is above the threshold, then check out your 401(k) plan and see if Roth contributions are allowed in your specific plan. (They usually are these days.) If they're available, you can allocate a portion or all of your deferral towards Roth in your 401(k). Any matching or profit sharing provided by your employer will *not* be considered

Roth money, but at least some or all of your contributions can go into Roth.

Finally, let's say your income is above the threshold for Roth contributions, and you don't have Roth provisions available to you in a 401(k) at work. You are allowed to convert any funds you have in IRAs to a Roth IRA. To convert, you simply transfer your investments from your IRA to a Roth. Simple, right? Wrong. Don't forget this transfer will be a taxable event. You will have to pay ordinary income tax on this transfer from your IRA to a Roth, so be careful. It's best to time Roth conversions in years when you can handle the taxes. It's not easy to find the right strategy for your specific situation, but it's worth the effort. Roth is a great retirement investment tool everyone should have in their toolbox. But what could be better?

What if we could put money in an account before tax *and* make money on it, tax free? Am I dreaming? I think not. This account exists, and it's called a health savings account, or HSA. These little gems were created years ago to help self-employed folks save money for their deductible when using a high deductible health plan. Since that time, the healthcare crisis in our country has continued to swell. Now, many Americans are either on or have available to them a high deductible health plan, just to keep premiums somewhere between astronomical and insane. If you are on a high-deductible health plan, then you are eligible for an HSA, whether through your work or individually.

Any contributions made to your HSA are made before taxes or are tax deductible. You may not know that you can invest the money in your HSA, and the returns are tax free. Interestingly, the tax incentive is tied to the *savings*, not the *use* of the money, so why use it now? Save your HSA contributions and invest them for retirement. There is one caveat: you must use the money in your HSA toward health-related expenses, like medical bills, prescriptions, long term care expenses, or insurance premiums. So what? As a financial planner, those are the expenses in retirement I am most worried about for my clients, so it makes sense to have a bucket of money dedicated to their cause.

For example, my dentist client years ago elected to purchase a high-deductible health plan for her family to save money on premiums. She was then eligible to set aside money into an HSA to cover the deductible and out of pocket amounts for any medical costs incurred before her insurance kicks in. The contributions she made into her HSA were not taxed at all. Because of the tax benefits, the dentist's advisor (me) said, "Hey, stop using your HSA for current medical expenses and invest it, that way you can earn tax-free returns on tax deductible contributions. You can't do that anywhere else." She did what I recommended, and there is a *lot* of money in her HSA now, ready and waiting to be deployed in retirement, when she and her husband will probably have more medical costs than ever. By the way, HSA funds can be used for medical and long-term care insurance premiums too.

So, I recommend you save as much as you can in your HSA, move it where it can be invested, and let it ride. If you're worried about having enough healthcare expenses in retirement to document against withdrawals, just keep a running tally of health-related expense. You can reimburse yourself at any time for these expenses, even if it's 30 years later.

Investment Expense: Don't Fund Your Advisor's Retirement at the Expense of Your Own

Besides taxes, another potential load that can drastically mitigate a steep time value of money curve is investment expense. We talked about how your real return is your return over the inflation rate, and we talked about how important it is to minimize taxes. Expenses are a load on our portfolio as well that directly reduce our return, just like inflation and taxes.

Some expenses are necessary, but many are not. Know what you are paying for. The easiest way to reduce expenses is to avoid working with commissioned salespeople. Many of their products have massive expenses associated with them and are carefully designed to be attractive to consumers but highly profitable for the financial services companies that market them. They make their products attractive by playing on those two human emotions that spell disaster for long term investors: fear and greed. If a salesman tells you they have a product that can provide market-level return with no downside, they are probably selling you a very high commission or cost investment vehicle to fund their *own* retirement, not yours. Run in the other direction.

If you are working with a fee-only fiduciary advisor, the expenses will be easier to identify and evaluate. You will pay your advisor either a fixed dollar amount, a percentage of assets, or a combination of the two. Similarly, you will either be paying for financial planning, portfolio management, or a combination as well. With the right advisor who is only registered to provide advice and not to sell investment or insurance products, you shouldn't have to worry about getting caught in a high-commission packaged product, but there are other expenses you need to be aware of.

First off, there are trading expenses. Each time you buy or sell a security or mutual fund, the activity potentially triggers a transaction charge by the clearing firm. The advisor either passes this on to you or absorbs it as part of what's called a wrap program. You'll want to know how much this charge is, how often to expect transactions, and who pays it. Generally, these expenses are very low, especially when the advisor is appropriately investing your money for the long term and using efficient trading and rebalancing strategies.

If your portfolio includes mutual funds, there will be expenses within your mutual funds. You won't see these expenses unless you look them up because your return is net of these fees. The mutual fund manager and all of the expenses associated with running the fund need to be paid by somebody, and that somebody is you. You should be aware of what these expenses are, since they come directly off the top before your return.

Finally, there could be additional expenses associated with a third-party money manager. These expenses would be layered between your mutual fund and trading expenses and your financial advisor's fee, like an Oreo cookie. Many financial advisors hire third-party managers to run their client's money. If the financial advisor is contracting the money management and making you pay for it, there should be a concession in there for what he charges, right? Make sure you know what the total expense is for all of the fees associated with your account, and make sure it makes sense to you.

Don't forget, fee-only fiduciary advisors, such as myself, are selling something too. We want to convince you to be our client and charge you a fee that is profitable for us. You need to evaluate what we have to offer and make sure you are paying a reasonable cost for something that's going to get you where you want to go financially. Just like I mentioned earlier, don't let your emotions of fear and greed get in the way of a good decision here.

If an advisor tells you they can get you out of the market before a big drop and back in again for the gains, run in the other direction. In highly efficient financial markets, this is simply not possible on a consistent, long-term basis. It's what every investor wants to hear, but flies in the face of the basic interrelationship between risk and return. Our magical time value of money process relies heavily upon the premise that if you take on risk with your money, over the long run you will reap a commensurate and fair return for that risk. Try to shortcut the magic, and your sorcery will create nothing but doom and gloom.

Chapter 3

DON'T BLAME YOUR DEBT, MANAGE YOUR CASH

As Americans, we are truly unique outliers compared to the rest of the world as it relates to financial independence. First off, a wide majority of humans still live in undeveloped regions and subsist at a very basic level, with no capability to save anything at all for their future. We are so fortunate to have the opportunity to plan and save for our future. Yet even in most other developed countries, the concept of saving for retirement is completely foreign. These countries have a more socialist tilt, so the government provides for retirement income at a much higher level than our Social Security system, albeit at a much greater tax burden.

I think our independent, pioneer heritage has created in us a deep desire for success, that American Dream. Our ancestors crossed oceans and plains at perilous risk in order to find a better way of life for themselves and their families. I believe that drive and desire is still there and is the reason for our nation's success as a world-leading economic power.

The good news is that our economic and political environments are set up relatively well for us to achieve and succeed. The bad news is this freedom comes with a high level of personal responsibility. I believe what you and I do with this freedom, whether we choose to be responsible or not, has grave consequences not only for ourselves but for future generations.

In order to maintain a nice living for our entire lifetime, we *must* save for our future. We have the tools and resources available to us to make this happen. As long as we don't procrastinate or be irresponsible with these tools and resources, the opportunity is ours. If, as a society, we fail at this, then the economic and political environment that makes it possible will go away, along with any chance of future generations to have the same opportunities we enjoy. And the best way to fail at all of this is to allow personal debt to get out of control.

Thanks to Dave Ramsey, there is more awareness about the hazards of consumer debt than there has ever been before. Yet, as a nation, we recently set an all-time record for consumer debt, as it topped $13.51 trillion in the 3rd quarter of 2018.[1]

What gives? Dave has done a great job bringing awareness to the consumer debt problem in America, but his advice is dangerously shortsighted. I think it's similar to the savings problem in that, if we fail to plan, there is no positive motivation for sound financial habits. Eliminating debt is not a goal, it's a step towards a goal. If all we focus on is eliminating debt, what does that really accomplish in terms of long-term financial success? If we don't have a sound plan, we have no idea what eliminating debt accomplishes. Rather, we're just bebopping along, cycling into debt, out of debt, and right back in again. That's what's happening across the country to Ramsey disciples because they are focusing on the wrong problem.

---

1   "Total Household Debt Rises for 17th Straight Quarter: New Research Shows Delinquency Rates Higher Among Younger Borrowers," *Federal Reserve Bank of New York*, November 16, 2018, https://www.newyorkfed.org/newsevents/news/research/2018/rp181116

When it comes to consumer debt, instead of just calling it evil and paying it down only to build it up again later, let's try to identify how we may have gotten there in the first place and make a plan from there. Consumer debt is usually the product of not having enough money available for a current want or need. That of course makes perfect sense. If there is not enough money available, therein lies the problem: inadequate cash savings. So, if all you're doing is paying down debt, you'll never get around to saving enough cash for the next emergency or opportunity, and you'll find yourself right back where you started.

The first step to breaking this cycle is to cultivate and maintain cash reserves. It'll help ensure you don't find yourself right back where you started. Think as if you were an accountant for a second. Accountants like balance sheets because they show all of your assets minus all of your liabilities. If the net result is a solid positive number, that's a good thing. All of our clients have balance sheets that we create for them demonstrating, over time, how their decisions around debt and savings affect their long-term financial health. If you pay down debt, that improves your net worth dollar for dollar on a balance sheet. But that's not the only way to improve your net worth. If you save more, your savings improves your net worth dollar for dollar too.

Now let's talk about the accountant's other little buddy: the cash flow statement. A cash flow statement is a lot like a budget, but more of a snapshot of what your sources of income are right now and your associated expenses on a monthly basis. Just like with the balance sheet, we are looking for a good positive net difference between income and expenses. We also produce these for our clients because cash flow either feeds or eats net worth. These two financial statements are interrelated in this way. If you are maintaining debt, it requires you to pay interest, so debt reduces cash flow and potentially erodes your long-term net worth. If you have investments, they should be providing positive cash flow, therefore improving your balance sheet. All of this works together to create a symphony of actions and reactions as you pull different levers to try and create positive financial results. Most healthy balance sheets, whether it's a company's balance sheet or family's personal balance sheet, maintain balances in all three categories: short-term cash, long-term investments, and debt.

It's important to understand that debt is not bad in and of itself. Debt is a financial instrument or tool that can be used properly to solve financial problems or improperly to create them. For example, all of the sudden, life starts to happen, and you and your spouse find yourselves with two small children living in the same apartment you rented when you were first married. You all need more space, and like any parent, you want to be somewhere that has a good elementary school for Junior and Sally. The right house in the right neighborhood is going to cost $280,000. Let's say the two of you are fantastic savers, and at the young age of 30, you have exactly $280,000 in savings and investments. Does it make sense to drain your investments and savings to purchase the home? Of course not. About $200,000 of the $280,000 is invested for the long term and making an average of 6% per year. That means this year it could throw off $12,000 in returns. If you put 20% down, that will still leave you with more than $20,000 in cash savings for emergencies. Then, if you get a 30-year mortgage at 3.45%, your payments will be right at $1,000 per month.

On your cash flow statement, the $12,000 in loan payments and $12,000 in return on long term investments is a wash, but that's now, this year. Over time, let's say you stay in the home until it's paid off at your age of 60. Each year, the investments you decided not to sell off to buy the house compound. At age 60, they are not producing a measly $12,000 in return anymore. Now it's potentially producing $72,000 in return because your $200,000 is now $1.2 million. Oh, and your house is paid off now too and has increased in value nicely. Using debt as a leverage tool, you're $1.2

million richer than you would have been if you cashed out your investments to stay debt free.

To be fair, if you had saved the $1,000 per month in mortgage payments at the same 6% over that 30-year period, you would still have around $1 million in investments. So technically, the mortgage leverage created $200,000 in net worth, not $1.2 million. But I don't know many families with young kids in a new house that would be able to force themselves to save the difference. You're much more likely to pay the mortgage.

As long as your cash flow can handle it, a mortgage is a great debt tool. In some cases, it may make sense to pay off your mortgage early, but paying the mortgage down early is not something I'm often concerned about with clients. If my client wants to purchase a second home with leverage, we may consider paying off the primary home just to keep the debt portion of the balance sheet in check.

Stepping further into our scenario, let's say you went ahead and took every dime of that $280,000 you have saved up and paid cash for the house. Dave Ramsey is proud of you when you call in on his radio show. But a few months go by, and some financial challenges arise. It doesn't matter what they are, whether medical related, major car repairs, temporary unemployment, you name it. They are the kind of challenges that you would have easily been able to handle with the $80,000 in cash you had in your savings account, but it's in your house now. So instead of $80,000 in cash, you all of the sudden have $80,000 in revolving credit card debt. Forgoing the mortgage at 3.5% now means you're paying 18% in credit card interest every month. That's $14,400 a year, more than the mortgage would have been, and that's just the interest alone.

Let's go back to where the problem with debt stems from and discuss it further. Remember, debt arises when there is not enough cash to meet current needs and wants. But our society wants you to believe people with poor character get themselves into debt, and those with good character and sound resolve are able to resist temptation and remain financially pure.

Hogwash. Character has little to do with it, and shaming or brow beating ourselves or those who are in debt doesn't help at all. In financial planning, we attack the problem, not the person. More than a few times, I've had couples reach out to me for financial planning help. Sometimes we find things aren't adding up, and they come clean about the debt issues pulling them down. They feel embarrassed or ashamed, but hiding those problems doesn't help them tackle the issue. At that point, we have to stop, back up, and begin again. It would have been easier for them in the long run had they just been honest about what was going on.

I have one client couple who lost a child years ago. They were devastated in a way I can only imagine. A dark period of depression followed, then job loss, and suffering ensued. Over the course of that time, they accumulated a large amount of debt. They worried it was insurmountable. But their lives were not over. Through their faith, hard work, and support of one another, they were able to dig themselves out. Today, they are living a happy, comfortable retirement together. Don't tell me they got into trouble with debt because they lacked character. This couple demonstrated strength of character in spades.

Whenever I find myself counseling someone who is challenged by their debt and ashamed about it, I talk to them about how they got there. We're usually able to identify key events and/or actions that created the problem. This helps us look at debt as a challenge or problem with a viable solution rather than a personal flaw. Life happens. There are circumstances beyond our control and sometimes we can only react and resolve. Financial planning is not the nice, neat, clean, and orderly process we sometimes make it out to be. Real life is full of twists and turns, surprises, problems, and tragedy. But through planning we can learn to mitigate challenges and capitalize on opportunities.

So how do we solve the problem of excess debt? I've found it almost solves itself if there is enough income available to slowly and steadily pay down debt while still maintaining good savings. Money can be deployed against credit cards and the like, as long as there's enough in savings to deal with all of the unexpected expenses that come up so often.

If cash flow is super tight, or negative, then you may be forced to sell off some investments, a car, or even your home in order to raise cash and pay down debt. Or, you can also create another income stream through a second job or improving the income potential of your current job. As humans, we are creative beings. I believe if we identify the problem, we can solve just about anything.

Sometimes, we have to tackle the problem of excessive spending to solve debt problems. The media really loves to harp on this one. In my experience, excessive spending is rarely the culprit. Most people who know they are in trouble with debt don't overspend. Occasionally, irrational behavior or some kind of addiction or dysfunction is to blame but not often. When overspending is to blame, the best solution is accountability. I strongly recommend you learn to be accountable to your spouse and/or to a financial planner. That way you won't be able to hide destructive behavior as easily, and you can deal with it accordingly. I review hundreds of cash flow budgets every year. Every once in a while, I'm able to help a couple find ways to cut spending, but like I said before, that's not usually the issue.

If cash flow feels tight and you don't have at least three months' worth of expenses in savings, you're in the danger zone. Your best course of action at this point is to force savings upon yourself. We'll talk more about how to do that in the cash chapter. Ideally, you can build up some cash before something goes awry. Try to automate everything you can so you're not constantly juggling and having to make decisions. Decide once how much you want to save automatically and give it a go. If it ends up being more than you can handle, adjust your savings downward and keep going.

Do the same with any revolving debt you want to retire. Find a number you think you can handle and throw that amount of cash at your credit card every month automatically, then forget about it. If all goes well, and it will if you are maintaining enough cash in the bank for emergencies, your debt will be gone before you know it.

Making Delayed Gratification Seem More Immediate

We have hashed out the problem of debt pretty well now and even discussed some solutions that work, but the best solution is good, long-term financial planning. We all suffer from a condition called short-term bias. Short-term bias means that, when we identify threats or opportunities, we give immediate or short-term threats and opportunities more credence than long-term ones, even if the long-term threats are more dire.

Back when humans lived in caves with saber-toothed tigers roaming about the countryside, I'm sure this short-term bias thing came in handy. The fella who ignored immediate short-term threats probably never got the chance to live out and implement a long-term plan of any kind. His tendencies and genes died off, and never made it into our genetic makeup. That's the theory, anyway.

This plays out to our detriment in a couple of ways when it comes to debt. One way is obvious. If I'm in the PGA Superstore and drop $637 onto my Visa card for a new PING G410 Plus Driver today, it's probably because I think it's going to gain me a stroke or two this Saturday morning with the boys. If I pick up a stroke or two on the golf course, I might win $10 in skins and greenies.

But next month when Shelly opens the credit card bill, we might have to have a serious discussion. Maybe I had promised we were going to get a new ice maker, and now I can't honor that promise. That's going to be a pain point, for sure. So, in order to relieve marital stress, let's say we go ahead with the new ice maker *and* the PING driver. Shelly needs good quality ice for the chai lattes she makes for herself just as badly as I need a new driver. Maybe that's more than our current cash flow will allow, so $637 gets carried on the credit card bill at 14% interest. I just did the math, and, at that interest rate, my driver costs almost $90 more if we carry that balance for one year. Ouch, that's a lot of skins on the golf course.

The other way short-term bias hurts us with debt is less obvious but critical to understand. If there is a debt problem, short-term bias encourages us to focus on the debt and nothing else. As we discussed previously, this kind of deep focus on one single financial problem puts us into a bad cycle. The correct way to approach debt is to understand how it fits, or doesn't fit, into our long-term financial goals. We make a plan and identify the long-term challenges that will HAVE to be addressed, like college for our kids and retirement. If you have $30,000 in revolving debt, maybe that's a big deal. But you may also have two kids starting college in the next four years or so that could easily cost $200,000. And if you ever want to retire, estimate needing roughly $4 million in today's dollars, and you might be in the ballpark of what's required. You probably don't have the resources to solve all three of these problems right now, so you have to prioritize them.

Which is most important? That's up to you. But we can easily argue that retirement savings is the biggest number, will require the most resources, and will have the greatest impact on you and your family. Short-term bias can prevent us from dealing with retirement early enough in our lives to have a good shot at accomplishing this important goal effectively. With a plan that provides us with an understanding of what important financial goals need to be met, we likely won't simply take all of our resources, time, and effort and pay down debt. Rather, we'd build up our cash reserves, maybe drip some money into the kids' college accounts, and maintain steady retirement plan contributions along with a long-term debt-paydown strategy. It will take longer to get the debt handled, but it is more likely to be handled for good since we are looking ahead and dealing with multiple financial goals simultaneously to develop a strong, diversified balance sheet.

The key to implementing a sound, well-rounded financial plan is automation. With automation, we make an initial decision on how much to allocate to these different pieces of our overall plan, go back to our busy, crazy lives, and forget about it for a while. A certain amount gets pulled from our check for retirement before we get paid; then a small portion is automatically set aside into our savings account. From there, an automatic payment is sent to our credit card company and another into the kids' college account. What's left is what we live on. Most families can make the adjustments needed to live on what's left, as long as it's a reasonable amount and as long as cash reserves are maintained for unexpected expenses. It's usually that simple and does not require much time and effort.

If you don't automate, you'll find yourself constantly fighting your short-term bias tendencies, having to make the same decisions over and over and over again. This is not a healthy approach. I'm sure there are people out there who can handle their finances this way. I'm not one of them. I would much rather automate, live my life, and revisit the planning again in six months or a year to make adjustments. That's what I recommend to clients.

The Good, the Bad, and the Ugly When It Comes to Debt

We've talked a little about mortgages and how they can be a good financial tool for a young family. We've also talked about credit cards, or revolving debt, and how it can sink you in a hurry. How do we recognize and distinguish good debt from bad debt? I think we can easily break it down in a few ways to better understand and utilize debt to our advantage.

- **Collateralized vs. Uncollateralized:** Collateral is a banking term that means a debt is backed by some kind of asset. Your mortgage is backed by the value of your home as collateral, just like a car loan is backed by the value of your car. Generally speaking, collateralized debt will have a lower interest rate associated with it, since there is less risk to the lender. It also means that your personal balance sheet will look stronger and healthier because there is an asset associated with your liability. We generally prefer collateralized debt over uncollateralized.

- **Appreciating vs. Depreciating:** When it comes to collateral, there are two types of assets in this world, appreciating assets and depreciating assets. If an asset that is purchased with debt appreciates, this means it increases in value over time. If the asset appreciates at a greater clip than the interest rate on the loan, then you effectively used debt as leverage and gained real dollars like a savvy tycoon. If your collateral depreciates, then the debt load adds to your losses or expenses on that asset over time. We like using debt on assets that have the potential to appreciate over time, like a house, better than we like debt on assets that depreciate over time, like a car.

- **Installment vs. Revolving:** Both an installment loan and a revolving loan can be collateralized or uncollateralized. When a debt revolves, it means it has no real beginning or end. A credit card revolves because it's always available and doesn't have a set-in-stone payment schedule. There may be a minimum payment, but usually, you can pay that minimum from now until the end of time and the debt will never retire. Installment loans have a set payment that includes principal and interest so that, over a set period of time, the debt pays off. We like installment loans better than revolving credit because they take care of themselves over time and usually carry a better interest rate.

Here is a matrix of some different types of credit and how they are characterized from better to worse:

Collateralized/Appreciating/Installment (e.g. home mortgage)
Collateralized/Depreciating/Installment (e.g. car loan)
Collateralized/Appreciating/Revolving (e.g. home equity line of credit to redo your kitchen)
Uncollateralized/Appreciating/Installment (e.g. student loan for your MBA)
Uncollateralized/Depreciating/Revolving (e.g. washer and dryer on a Best Buy credit card)

A Quick Word on Credit Scoring

For most established families, credit scoring should not be an issue. Pay your bills on time, and you should not have to worry too much about your credit score. Unlike what you may think, credit scores don't necessarily score you based upon how good you are with credit. Rather, they score you on how good of a target you are for credit. This means there are people who pay their bills on time with good incomes that have mediocre credit scores. Why? It's because they don't access credit much and, therefore, are not a good target for credit card companies.

When shopping for a car loan or mortgage, there will usually be little to no difference in the interest rate you receive as long as your credit is "above average," "good," or generally above 700 on a FICO scale. It's good to monitor your credit so you know where you stand and also to mitigate fraud or identity theft. But don't agonize over it. If your credit score is 710, and you have nice, healthy savings and investments, you are much better off than your neighbor with an 810 score and no retirement savings. Focus on building your assets, not your credit score, and you'll be better off in the long run.

WHEN *NOT* TO PAY OFF A DEBT

Believe it or not, there are certain instances where you should not pay off a debt. It's not uncommon at all for a debt to go delinquent on you without your knowledge. This most commonly occurs with medical bills. Don't get me started, but medical billing in this country is a complete mess and has been for years and years.

Case in point, my daughter broke her hand in a car accident in 2010, went to the emergency room, and subsequently had surgery. We waded through all of the bills and insurance statements, paid our deductible, and moved on. In 2017, my son dislocated his shoulder playing football, and we ended up in the same emergency room. Along with all of the bills associated with Daniel's injury, the visit must have triggered something somewhere because we got a bill for over two grand from a collection firm associated with Gretchen's emergency room visit seven years earlier. Before paying it, Shelly went to the hospital and had them look it up. The hospital had no record of us owing anything. Shelly called and explained this to the collection agency, but they didn't care. They said we owed it, but they would be more than happy to take any amount we could afford over regular monthly installments to satisfy the claim.

Hell no. First of all, to my knowledge, the debt never made it to the credit bureaus, and if it had, after seven years it falls off and cannot be reported any longer. But, if we had agreed to paying a reduced amount or installments, legally the bad debt could be refreshed and reported going forward, for seven more years. Second of all, we didn't owe it.

So, by now you should see a trend that will continue throughout this book. If we are going to be financially successful, we have to learn to work on multiple financial goals, all at the same time. If we focus too much on one thing, like debt, then *whack*, we'll get popped in the face by something else eventually, with no resources to deal with it effectively. Clients often ask me if they should do this or that, such as pay off a credit card or put money in a college fund. My answer is usually, "Yes." Both answers are correct. Because of the time value of money continuum that we discussed last chapter, we just don't have enough time to put stuff off. We have to deal with all of it simultaneously to be most effective. It's hard to do but not impossible, and the real key to making it all work is a good, solid cash reserve.

Chapter 4

CASH MONEY. BLING. BUCKETS.

Cold hard cash is hands down your most important asset, and that is the hardest lesson to teach. Many people don't realize this when they start investing, and it really screws things up. If there were a pyramid of assets, cash would be the base of the pyramid. Without cash, there is nothing to hold up and protect all of your investments. If you don't maintain adequate cash reserves, you're going to be sorry at some point. Or, you're going to miss out on a great opportunity.

MY CASH MENTOR

Years ago, I headed to an early morning event with my mentor Noel Blaas. We were in his brand-new Land Rover, and I, being the young knucklehead that I was, just spilled an entire cup of Whataburger coffee all over myself and his leather seats. Noel was on top of his game. He was a very successful career life insurance agent, well known throughout the entire continent for his consistently high level of production. At the time, we both sold long-term financial products, like life insurance and mutual funds. Noel had raised and educated his kids and was on the verge of retiring. I had just completed my second year in the industry and broke out with some decent, award-winning production numbers myself. My success gave me the opportunity to plan.

"Hey, Noel, I'm socking away a good amount this year towards my kids' college funds and retirement. Is there anything else you think I should be doing?" Noel replied in his usual dead-serious, direct, Midwestern way, "Cash, cold hard cash. Your most important asset is cash. Without cash, your other assets are just hanging in the wind. Get your cash in line first, then start building from there." I'm surprised he took my question seriously with coffee still dripping off my pants onto his seats like I had wet myself.

His response surprised me in other ways too. It didn't fit with any of the sales training I completed nor what I had experienced thus far in my young life. But fast forward a quarter of a century, and I know *exactly* what he was talking about. No matter how successful you are, there are times when things don't go as planned. If you don't have cash when the unexpected occurs, you must either take on leverage or liquidate long-term assets. Neither of which benefits your financial future.

Prior to my conversation with Noel, I had already learned how cash savings provide opportunity. Fresh out of college and newly married, I entered the Navy as a young ensign in 1990. The Navy provided Shelly and me with the opportunity to buy series EE bonds, which are, in essence, a cash equivalent. Series EE bonds make a paltry, low interest, guaranteed return with the US Treasury. But in spite of this, we decided to have a very small amount deducted out of each of my very small paychecks. We barely even noticed the deductions. The bonds accumulated and were physically held by the Navy for our benefit. We never saw the bonds or even knew how to access them, and pretty much forgot they were there. Four years later, I had resigned my commission, and we were starting a new life and career in Mansfield, Texas. We had decided to build a house for our growing family and were trying to decide on a feasible way to come up with the down payment.

Almost on cue, one day I received a big, thick package in the mail from the US Navy Bureau of Personnel in Cleveland, Ohio. I opened the package to find a giant stack of all of the Series EE bonds that had accumulated over my four years in the Navy. What a great deal! That was my opportunity, at a very young age, to buy a house and put 20% down for it. It wouldn't have happened without the cash available from years of regular automatic deductions. I see young people all the time struggling to come up with a down payment for their first home. I agree with Noel: young people should start a forced savings plan for cash first then build from there.

I know that in my life and career, there have been ups and downs, and cash is what kept us going when things got tough. Cash is what allows us to continue to take care of our family when bad things happen or take advantage of opportunities, like buying a house or an opportune investment when the time is right.

How Much Cash?

How much cash should you have on hand? It depends. I wish there was a general rule that applied to everybody, but there's not. Everybody is different, with their own life experiences, risks, and opportunities, and, therefore, their own unique cash needs. If you don't know where to start, then try to save up three months of expenses, then up it to six months' worth.

If you've been at this for a while, you probably already know how much cash a comfortable amount is based upon your experiences. For Shelly and me, it was again during our time as young parents while I was in the Navy when we had our most memorable experience around cash needs. My ship conducted a homeport change from Norfolk, Virginia to Charleston, South Carolina just after our first child, Gretchen, had entered the world. In standard Navy fashion, the homeport change, along with all of the personal logistics associated with moving our families, became a low priority compared to the need to train and qualify for our upcoming deployment. So, instead of weighing anchor and just moving the ship down the coastline, we stayed at sea for six weeks training while our families moved on their own. The move was brutal for Shelly, who was alone with an infant, but to make matters worse, we did not get a single paycheck for those six weeks. There was a glitch in my payroll that only I could personally resolve, but I was at sea. (This was before email and cell phones, so I was not accessible in any way.) Shelly had just enough money to buy formula and peanut butter. Unbeknownst to me, my wife and new baby slept in a sleeping bag on the floor in our new place without any furniture or utilities for most of that six-week period.

Use your own experiences and instincts to come up with a cash goal that feels comfortable. For some, it's $50,000 and for others, it may be $5,000. But I encourage you not to think of your cash goal as a single number but, rather, as a range. Starting off, you may want to think of that range in terms of monthly expenses. Maybe you think having three-to-six months of expenses socked away sounds right. If you don't know what your monthly expenses are, that's okay. Use this simple worksheet as a guide for coming up with your monthly expense estimate and necessary range for savings (*larger image of worksheet available in the end chapter of book*).

Item	Per Month	Per Annum	Item	Per Month	Per Annum
LOANS & LIABILITIES			OTHER LIVING COSTS		
Mortgage			Childcare		
2nd or HELOC			Clothing		
Home/Property Insurance			School/ University Fees		
HOA Dues			Allowance		
Property Tax					
Personal Loans			Clothes/Shoes - Personal		
Auto Lease			Entertainment/ Restaurants		
Auto Loan			Gym/Club Membership		
Investment Loans			Sports & Fitness		
Credit Cards			Furniture/Appliances		
Life Insurance			Books		
Income Protection			Pet Costs		
Other			Netflix/Amazon Subscriptions		
TOTAL:	$0.00	$0.00	Gifts/Donations		
			Lunch/Coffee		
			Holidays		
HOME, UTILITY, HEALTH			Travel		
Rent			Other		
Water			TOTAL:	$0.00	$0.00
Electricity					
Gas					
Cable/SAT TV			TRANSPORTATION		
Home Phone			Car Insurance		
Mobile Phone			Car Fuel		
Internet			Car Repairs & Maintenance		
Home Maintenance			Transport Costs (Bus, etc.)		
Household Help			Other		
Yard Maintenance			TOTAL:	$0.00	$0.00
Groceries					
Medical/Dental Consultations					
Private Health Insurance					
Pharmacy/ Prescriptions			Accountant		
Other			Attorney		
TOTAL:	$0.00	$0.00			

Now, visualize a bucket filled with water with two marks on the bucket. One mark is called the high-water mark, and the other is the low-water mark. Ask yourself, "How much cash is too much?" In other words, let's say, for instance, you have come up with $40,000 as the high-water mark, but your savings exceed this amount. Some of the excess money could be deployed better towards important long-term goals, right? So, you siphon it off into another bucket, like your kids' college fund or retirement. Now ask yourself, "How much cash is too little?" If $20,000 is your low-water mark, and your cash gets below $20,000, start finding ways to save money and fill your bucket back up.

Sounds easy, right? All we have to do is manage our cash between the high-water and low-water marks, and we're good to go. Well, for most of us, it's not that easy. The cash we accumulate represents the opportunity for immediate gratification with *lots* of wants and needs that we all experience every day. Human nature is not on our side when it comes to maintaining cash reserves, so here are some ways to trick ourselves into doing what's best for our financial success.

TRICKS FOR SAVING CASH

"Anything in the checking account, consider it gone." Alan Phillips, one of my best friends said this years ago in one of our client meetings. I think a majority of seasoned savers would agree with this statement, and most who don't agree are just kidding themselves. So many people try over and over and over again to save money in their checking accounts to the point of exasperation. I say give up. Just let it go. Like Alan says, consider any money that hits the checking account gone.

If we are going to save cash, we ideally want to make it happen before our paycheck ever hits our checking account. Remember the Series EE bonds I purchased in the Navy? Those worked for Shelly and me because they were automatic. We didn't have to think about it. We made one decision, and it lasted four years. I can assure you, if I had been asked by the Navy at each pay period, "Hey, Rob, we're going to take $25 dollars out of your check. Are you okay with that?" more often than not, we would have opted out due to this expense, or that need, or whatever. These days, just about everybody has the ability to split their paycheck and have a portion allocated to a savings account. If you are not taking advantage, do it now. Don't put it off. Just make the decision once, and your future self will be grateful.

In the personal financial world, there are net spenders and net savers. Net spenders *pay* interest. Net savers *make* interest. Net spenders can never seem to catch a break. The car breaks down or needs tires, or a large medical expense pops up out of nowhere. And *boom*, the net spender just falls behind even more. The net spender usually is oblivious to the real reason for their financial woes; they think it's their circumstances, not their financial habits, that are to blame. To the contrary, the net saver experiences many of the same hardships but is able to adequately handle these expenses with cash savings. Same circumstances, but the net saver feels blessed that they had the resources available to handle their circumstances Rarely does the net saver realize how important their saving habits were to the pleasant financial outcome they experienced when under duress.

If you are a net spender, understand that the inertia of your financial habits is going to be very hard to overcome, and it may take a while. Regardless, the first step is to start saving cash reserves. The first step is *not* to pay down debt with every extra penny you have. You may need car tires, or maybe shoulder surgery, or something in the near future. If you don't have cash savings, all that debt paydown was for nothing, and the endless debtor cycle will continue with no end in sight.

I know it's sad to think of it this way. But there are people who learn how to achieve financial success, and there are those who never achieve financial success. Certainly, circumstances come into play. But let's be honest; it really just comes down to whether or not we spend more than we make or make more than we spend. If you set up an automatic cash savings plan, you are much more likely to make more than you spend, so do it now.

More Tricks

We'll discuss next why banks are the best place for us to keep our cash reserves, but it's important that we make sure our accounts are set up on our terms, not the industry's terms. Banks are not providing us with the opportunity to save out of altruism. It's for their profit. They are going to provide a ridiculously low rate of interest. Besides laddered CDs or government instruments like we will discuss later, we don't have much choice but to accept the paltry, low interest they provide. But when you opened that savings account, guess what? They probably signed you up for automatic overdraft protection. Overdraft protection sounds great, but basically it just makes your savings account an extension of your checking account. I say reject the automatic overdraft and just make darn sure that you don't spend more than what's in your checking account. Otherwise, you may become over-dependent upon the automatic overdraft protection, thus deep-sixing your savings plans.

In addition, if you set up your savings account at the same bank as your checking, it will be linked in your internet connection, allowing you to transfer money whimsically from your smartphone, anywhere in the world. Sounds great, doesn't it? Some people can handle this level of accessibility and others cannot. Know thyself. For the record, I can't handle this level of accessibility. This does not make me a bad, immoral, or financially incompetent person. I'm just human, and I like all sorts of cool gadgets and equipment for all of my various hobbies and interests.

Put a buffer between you and your cash savings. If your savings are at the same bank, opt out of internet access to the savings, so you have to physically go into the bank to get your money. Better yet, put your savings in another bank. Years ago, I was struggling with cash savings, so I opened a savings account at the sleepiest, most low-tech credit union in town. I had no access to my savings except at the teller window during banking hours. That worked.

Building a good financial foundation is much more about creating the right habits and processes than it is about effectively curbing our daily needs and wants. Let's say you wake up today and have $3,000 of additional cash just sitting in your checking account. It's just *asking* to be instantly morphed into a [insert desire here]. (Mine right now is a DEWALT DW735 heavy-duty 13" Three Knife, Two Speed Thickness Planer.) You can probably resist because maybe you're really good at this Puritan denial thing. You're so good at it that you wake up 364 times this year and make the same correct decision. But on that 365th day, for whatever reason, that planer is calling your name, and you click "buy now" on Amazon before another thought enters your head. There is no reason to put ourselves through such a ridiculous daily trial of denial, none whatsoever. Billions of dollars of marketing and advertising is being spent to create in us impulsive wants, and it's being spent because it works. Give yourself a break and set savings aside in a fairly inaccessible account.

Where and Where Not to Keep Cash

So, let's talk about where to keep cash and where *not* to keep cash. Don't keep cash just lying around the house, even in a safe or hidden somewhere "safe" in your home. Why? Well, if your house burns down, you just lost your house *and* all of your cash savings, right when you needed it most. If someone robs you, cash is generally not covered to any significant level on your homeowner's policy. Are you the type who loses your car keys from time to time? (I am; I admit it.) If so, you are in grave danger of hiding cash money from yourself too. These are real risks you take when you maintain your reserves as cash at home.

45

I know some people like to maintain their safety reserves as gold or gold coins. Personally, I think this is a terrible idea, but it depends on your worldview, I suppose. If you keep gold in lieu of cash and it's in your home, your gold is subject to the same risks I mentioned above. It could even put your life at risk if you have a large amount and the wrong people know about it. Gold is not only subject to loss but also to wild and volatile fluctuations in value. These fluctuations in value are primarily what make gold a terrible cash equivalent. Did I say, "cash equivalent?" Gold is *not* a cash equivalent at all. It's a commodity and, therefore, cannot be relied upon in a pinch. Those who like gold as a safe asset are relying on information that's just not relevant anymore. At one point our country's currency (among others) was based upon a gold standard, meaning it was backed by gold. Those days are long gone. There is no link between gold and US currency anymore; they are in two completely different asset classes that are not correlated in any way. Good luck buying even a stick of gum at the convenience store with gold; it's just not a reliable exchange instrument.

Back to my worldview comment: if you are concerned about the "last days" and prepping for "the fall," that's a whole other issue. Neither I nor anybody else can recommend how to prepare for a catastrophic event like World War III, nuclear fallout, zombies, or whatever else may be out there. Financial planning software cannot model apocalyptic scenarios. We all bring our own life experiences, opinions, and biases to the table when we plan for the future. If your primary concerns about the future include surviving a nuclear attack or an overthrow of the US government, then very little of the advice in this book is beneficial to you. All of the financial planning assumptions, market risk recommendations, and advice doled out here assume a stable and viable US government, drinking water safe from nuclear contamination, and zombie-free work commutes.

Seriously, we all worry about bad things happening. It's in our nature. So, one of the primary reasons to plan our financial future is to be worry free. I encourage you to not worry about rare catastrophic events you have no control over and, therefore, cannot plan against. Rather, make a plan and take actionable steps to prepare for things you *can* be prepared for and that are within the realm of possibility. Cash is your first step to being worry free.

So, where *do* we keep cash? In the bank, of course. Cash savings in a bank account is Federal Deposit Insurance Corporation (FDIC)–insured up to levels far beyond what most families will need. The FDIC is an independent government agency, meaning the guarantee is backed by the US federal government. Really, it's more complicated than that, but the guarantee is about as strong of a guarantee as we're going to get. It's stronger than those backed by large financial services firms in other financial products, like annuities, life insurance, or debentures (bonds). Brokerage accounts have large insured limits of protection against your brokerage firm failing, but it's not the "blanket" coverage that FDIC-insured funds provide. The bottom line is keep your cash reserves in the bank because it's the safest (up to the FDIC limit) and easiest to access.

"Which bank?" you might ask. That's totally up to you. Some prefer the big banks due to the accessibility and breadth of services. Others prefer smaller community banks or credit unions because they provide a sense of belonging and more opportunity for relationship building. Finally, there are online banks that strip out all of the expenses associated with brick-and-mortar operations to provide lower fees and better interest rates. There are lots of options, just pick what is comfortable for you and provides the services you value.

These days, when you maintain cash reserves, the return on your money is downright depressing, and as I mentioned before, there is not much you can do about it. Any decent amount of return on cash requires you to give up some liquidity, like for instance if you purchase a Certificate of Deposit (CD). A CD is a short-term note, whereby you agree to allow the bank to tie up your money for a specified period of time for a specific interest rate. You can purchase CDs (which are also FDIC insured, by the way) in monthly or yearly increments. In the right interest-rate environment, I've used CDs to maintain cash reserves very effectively in a ladder strategy.

A ladder is a way to give up liquidity without giving up liquidity. What I mean is, let's say you buy a six-month CD every month for six months. When you get to the sixth month, you now have access to the first CD you bought, and every month thereafter, you have a CD maturing and providing liquidity if you need it. Imagine you're climbing a ladder, as your left foot leaves the bottom rung, your right hand is reaching for the highest rung. Your left foot represents a CD maturing this June, and your right hand represents buying a new CD for another six months. All of the rungs between your lowest foot and highest hand represent the CDs you currently hold, all "laddered" out over the next six months.

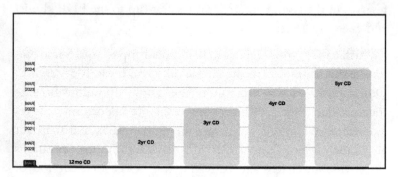

https://www.ally.com/do-it-right/banking/cd-laddering-how-to-build-a-cd-ladder/

In some interest-rate environments you can get a little better return on your cash using a short term ladder. But other times, you have to reach out a little farther to get a decent rate, maybe as far as five years or so. Of course, that's too long for cash reserves, but you can purchase CDs for that length, then use them as collateral for a line of credit with the bank. For most banks, a collateralized line against CDs held by the same bank should be at a very low interest rate, so low, you could use your line of credit *as* your cash reserve. The availability of funds comes at a cost, which is the net of the CD interest rate and the loan interest rate. For example, if you can get an average of 2.5% on your CDs and your line of credit interest rate is 4.5%, then the net cost of funds is 2% of whatever you may need to borrow. The kicker is, as long as you don't access the line of credit, it costs you nothing.

Other near-cash equivalents worth noting are Series I bonds and Treasuries. Series I bonds are a better, more modern version of the Series EE bonds I bought while in the Navy. You can buy them directly from the US Treasury at TreasuryDirect.gov, up to $10,000 worth per year. At TreasuryDirect.gov, you can also purchase T-bills and Treasury notes. T-Bills are bonds that mature in less than a year, and Treasury notes can be had in terms of two, three, five, seven, and ten years. You can ladder T-bills and Treasury notes in the same way as you can CDs, and you can use them as collateral for a low-interest line of credit with your bank.

Which brings us to an interesting question: can credit be used in lieu of cash reserves? The answer is maybe, at least partially. I don't think you should rely on credit as your primary cash reserves, but the right kind of credit can be used as a secondary cash reserve. For example, here in Texas, our property taxes are fairly high, and they are due at the end of every year. They are a common annual cash need. The best way to plan for annual property taxes, or other recurring large cash needs, is to just save up the cash and pay when due. On the other hand, there are other cash needs that come up irregularly and are fairly unknown as to their severity, like losing your job or a long illness. For these circumstances, a good lending source that has already been setup can be an excellent resource. (Trying to get a loan *after* losing your job is usually a non-starter.)

You can use the collateralized line of credit strategy already discussed with CDs or Treasury notes for emergency access to cash, or there are other good sources. If you have equity in your home, you can access it through a home equity line of credit, or HELOC. Just like the CD line of credit, you can set it up and forget about it. Then, if you need the cash, you can access the line at a low interest rate. Once you're past your cash emergency, you'll want to pay down the line and eliminate the debt.

You can also loan yourself money from a cash value life insurance policy. If you have a life insurance policy that has a cash value in it, you can access the cash by taking a loan against your policy. Just like the CD line strategy, your cost of funds is the net of the dividends and loan rate, which is generally very low. Again, you'll want to pay off the loan on your policy once your cash need has subsided, otherwise the interest will compound over time and possibly lapse your policy.

Finally, another common way to access cash in an emergency is to take a loan off your 401(k) balance. Not all 401(k) plan sponsors allow loans, but most do. Personally, I think we all should avoid 401(k) loans like the plague and use other resources for emergency cash. 401(k) loans are notoriously inflexible. Usually, the plan sponsor puts you on a five-year payoff that is hard to deviate from, and if you change jobs during that period, the loan is called due and netted out of your retirement assets with taxes and penalties. Finally, I just think it's a good idea to think of retirement funds *only* for retirement because that's when we'll need more money than at any other time in our lives.

Revolving Credit

Don't rely on revolving credit as emergency reserves unless you absolutely must. The interest rate on revolving debt will be two

50

to four times the rate on collateralized bank loans. That kind of interest load makes it very difficult to dig yourself out once the crisis has passed. Next thing you know, you're in the next crisis, and not only do you not have accessible funds but now you also have monthly credit card payments hanging on your back. Relying on revolving credit as reserves is basically the exact *opposite* of what we're trying to accomplish, so don't do it.

FINDING CASH TO SAVE: THE "B" WORD

In order to save cash, sometimes we have to find it, and the only way to find cash I know of is to create a cash flow statement, otherwise known as a budget. I've brought up the word "budget" with couples in client meetings from time to time and just watched as one or the other spouse cringes at the thought of such a painful ordeal. We generally marry somebody who's a little bit different than we are. So, when I'm planning with a couple, there's often one spouse who's really into budgeting and tracking every single penny that's ever been spent. The other spouse may be more of a free spirited, big picture person. I think both approaches have their merits and their faults, so it's critical to approach spending and tracking in a way that fits both personality traits. Otherwise, you have a great recipe for mistrust and resentment.

I think it's a mistake to try and track every single dollar you spend every month. That's not a budget. I don't know what it is, but it's not living a very fulfilled life. If you're tracking spending all of the time, you're focusing on the wrong thing. You know the mind experiment where somebody says, "Whatever you do, don't think of a pink elephant," and all of the sudden, your mind is flooded with pink elephants? If you focus too much on your spending, all you'll end up doing is spending because that's what you're thinking about.

On the other hand, never having a clue where your money goes is not a good approach either. If you don't know, you can't align your spending with your values. Is coffee a top priority in your life? (It is in mine. I'm fully caffeinated at all times.) If not, and you have no idea how much you are spending at Starbucks, how on earth can you determine that your spending is in line with your values?

Personal financial budgeting is about snapshots. It's good to go back, from time to time, and review a month of spending to see where your money went. You may find some surprises. "Holy cow, we spent $455 at Starbucks?" There it is, clear as day. Spending almost $500 per month at the coffee shop may not sit well with your values and what you deem to be reasonable. Mission accomplished. Now you *know* your spending was not in line with your values. In my experience, once you know, it's easy to make adjustments.

In client meetings, we'll go through a cash flow exercise where we just talk through the expense categories and come up with best guesses for what those expenses are going to be in the coming year. It doesn't have to be perfect. When we conduct a budget session, we're not necessarily trying to find ways to save, we're just trying to understand what the burn rate is. We call it the burn rate because that's what it feels like. The money we spend each month just burns away, never to be seen again. That's okay, as long as it provides us with food, shelter, clothing, entertainment, and so forth, but the burn has to be controlled so that it doesn't become an all-out forest fire.

In my experience with most families, the burn rate kind of is what it is. We all have established spending patterns. The basis of a cash flow statement is, of course, your income minus your expenses. Once you then subtract your taxes, we're hoping for a positive number. If you have a positive number, this means you have positive cash flow before savings, so you have the opportunity to save.

When we do this exercise, most people, unless they have overextended themselves on credit, have a positive cash flow before savings. Then, the question becomes, "Hey, where's that extra money going?" Answer: into the fire. Remember what my friend Alan said? "Consider it gone." The primary reason for the budget is to identify this positive cash flow before savings, so we can capture it and use it effectively in our financial plan. As you can see, budgeting is best done with a little bit of an eye to detail and a little bit of big picture thinking; it takes both.

So, we found it, captured it. Now what? Remember that I said most people, unless they are over-leveraged, will find themselves with extra money each month to put toward goals? Well, the flipside is that the extra is usually not a sufficient amount to accomplish everything we want. It's true. Calculate out how much you need to save for a comfortable retirement, and it's going to be a good chunk of what you have left over after monthly expenses. Add in a couple of kids with college aspirations, and that usually exceeds the available free cash flow. And didn't I say you need cash savings too?

Peeking over the Horizon

We'll spend all of our excess cash flow on a home remodel, not realizing what that's costing us as far as our ability to achieve financial independence someday. Or we go buy a car we really can't afford because we think of it based upon the payments, but those payments keep us from being able to make the contributions we would need in order to successfully educate our kids. Maybe we get really good at saving cash, but the return on cash is not sufficient for any of our long-term goals. So, it just sits there, eroding each day to inflation. It's important to peek over the horizon.

Danger Zone

If we keep pushing off our long-term goals, primarily retirement, then guess what happens. All of that cool time value of money magic we learned about never gets an opportunity to go to work for us. If you're saving money to put 20% down on a home, that's a big goal, but we must understand the amount of money needed to live when we are no longer working is easily 100 times the amount needed to purchase a home. It's hard to get our arms around how big our long-term goals are.

LITTLE DUTCH BOY AND THE DIKE

By far one of my favorite childhood stories is found in *Hans Brinker; or, the Silver Skates: A Story of Life in Holland* by Mary Mapes Dodge. It's about a little boy who saved the town of Haarlem by plugging holes he discovered in the dike with his fingers. That's what personal finance feels like. We identify one financial goal and plug it. Then another forms, and we plug it as well. Then another. Next thing we know, we have money allocated in several different directions. Some of the holes are large, maybe even leaking a little. Others may not be plugged at all yet, but we have an eye on them. In the midst of it, we're not sure if we're making much of a difference at all. But we *are*.

Smartly spreading our resources across our goals is the right way to approach the problem. I tell young parents all the time, "I know you can't save as much as you want for your kids' college, but anything you save, you'll be grateful you did". Making some progress is better than making no progress at all. Any amount of resources available at the time of a financial need, whether it's an emergency, college, retirement, or anything else, provides options.

SIGHTING

I used to do a lot of open water swimming. When you are swimming in a lake, river, or ocean, you can't see where you are going, and nobody swims in a straight line. Some swimmers have a tendency to veer right, others left, and still others may randomly zigzag. In order to make sure you are headed in the right direction, every few strokes, you must "sight."

This means you lift your head up above the waves just long enough to find the buoy or landmark you are swimming toward, so you can adjust your heading. If you sight on every stroke, you'll never get there because lifting your head takes extra effort and robs momentum. Likewise, if you never lifted your head, there's no telling where you would end up.

In our busy lives, we are all swimming to a distant buoy. No matter how hard or fast we work and save, if we don't lift up our heads from time to time and adjust our headings, we'll never get there. Then, once down in the water again, we can make progress. That's planning done the right way. To do this well, you'll need a financial planner, not a financial salesman. We'll discuss how to tell the difference in the next chapter.

Chapter 5

WHO'S WHO IN THE ZOO? A PLAIN ENGLISH EXPLANATION OF THE PLAYERS IN THE MONEY WORLD

Just How Big Is the Financial Universe Anyway?

There's big money in the financial services industry. When I say big, I mean really big, as in bigger than anything the world has ever seen. It's a universe all unto itself. Nearly all large corporations trade as a stock on the stock market, and those that don't still rely on some sort of financing or funding, privately or otherwise, that falls squarely into the behemoth financial services industry. All of the expensive spots during televised sports events, paid programming on Saturday morning radio, and massive media conglomerates (Bloomberg, WSJ, Forbes, CNBC) that are all dedicated to providing investment and finance information should tell us something.

There are two parts to the financial industry: B to B and B to C. Banks, insurance companies, pension funds, and other financial institutions trade with each other at a frantic, high-volume pace and with extreme efficiency. These folks know what they're doing and know the folks on the other side of the table know what *they* are doing. We call this B to B (business to business), and this part of the industry hums along efficiently behind the scenes with very little fanfare or media attention. Then there's B to C (business to consumer), and this is where it gets interesting. It should come as no surprise that the largest margins to be had in the financial sector are in the B to C segment. It's been estimated that over 17 billion dollars[2] in excess fees and expenses are charged to consumers by financial services companies every year just in IRAs alone. When I use the term "excess," what I mean are fees that savvy industry insiders and veterans (i.e. B to B professionals) know how to avoid.

Excessive investment expenses will directly affect your investment performance, which can steer you off course. Even more detrimental to consumers is the fact that these excess fees drive the industry to aggressively pursue you as a customer through their marketing, advertising, and salespeople. If you want to be financially successful, you have to know how to avoid these excess fees and expenses, and the easiest way to avoid them is to avoid the companies and salespeople who charge them.

In this B to C world, it's really difficult to tell who is who, who they work for, and what kinds of products they are selling. Because of the complexity, we need to go over who's who, what their roles are, and if they are necessary in your quest for financial security. Without better understanding, it's easy to fall prey to the salespeople of the industry or the emotional angst of the media or to just let everything fall by the wayside as you struggle to find the time on weekends and after work to try to manage your investments on your own.

Alphabet Soup

In my industry, as in many others, designations are used by advisors to learn and demonstrate their qualifications. These can be complicated. There are a couple of things you need to know about designations. Most designations are not licenses; rather, they are usually governed and administered by some separate, non-govern-

2   "The Effects of Conflicted Investment Advice on Retirement Savings," Executive Office of the President of the United States, February 2015, https://obamawhitehouse. archives.gov/sites/default/files/docs/cea_coi_report_final.pdf

ment entity. Secondly, just because an advisor has a designation does not necessarily mean he or she is looking out for your best interests. For instance, a CERTIFIED FINANCIAL PLANNER™, or CFP® professional, can receive commissions on sales of products all day long, so don't use this as your sole screening criteria. Always ask clear, specific questions.

But the most common designation for a financial planner or investment advisor *is* the CFP®. I have a couple of decades of experience in the realm of CFP® practitioners, and I believe it to be excellent training for providing sound financial advice to consumers. The CFP® certification has been around for over 45 years and has been managed by the same organizational structure, Certified Financial Planner Board of Standards, Inc. (CFP Board), since 1985. A CFP® must meet minimal education requirements that include a bachelor's degree and completion of either college-level, self-study, or classroom equivalent education in the following principal topics:

- Professional Conduct and Regulation
- General Principles of Financial Planning
- Education Planning
- Risk Management and Insurance Planning
- Investment Planning
- Tax Planning
- Retirement Savings and Income Planning
- Estate Planning

After completing the coursework or equivalent education requirements, they must pass a comprehensive examination. The CFP® exam is given three times per year and is a difficult, six-hour long, 170-question, computer-based test. The pass rate generally ranges between 50% and 60%. On average, a candidate studies around 1,000 hours for the exam. In addition to passing the exam, candidates must document 6,000 standard hours of experience "acquired through a variety of activities and professional settings including personal delivery, supervision, direct support, indirect support or teaching," according to the CFP Board website. Finally, a CFP® certificant must uphold the ethics outlined by the CFP Board in their Standard of Professional Conduct. If they don't, the certificant can get their designation suspended or revoked. Certificants also have to do 30 hours of continuing education every two years.

Another highly regarded designation is the Chartered Financial Analyst, or CFA. The CFA Institute acts as the governing body for what many consider to be the most difficult and arduous designation in the financial services industry. CFA candidates must attain 4,000 hours of specific work experience "[a]pplying or evaluating economic, financial, and/or statistical data in making investment decisions about securities or similar investments" prior to obtaining a CFA charter.[3] A bachelor's degree is also required, but it's the CFA education and testing process that really makes this designation tough.

There are three exams, called Level I, Level II, and Level III. Each exam coincides with a self-study, graduate-level curriculum comprised of 18 sections. The pass rate for each section historically hovers right around or just under 50%, but since you have to pass them in order of succession, the completion rate from Level I through Level III is a miniscule 12.9%.

CFA's are *the* investment experts in my industry, in my humble opinion. As such, many gravitate more toward being analysts and portfolio managers at large institutions. That being said, the curriculum fits extremely well with the knowledge and skills needed for personal portfolio management, so CFAs make great financial advisors.

3   "Work Experience Guide," CFA Institute, accessed January 30, 2020, https://www.cfainstitute.org/membership/join/work-experience

Finally, there is the Chartered Financial Consultant, or ChFC, credential that can be attained through self-study material and testing provided and administered by the American College. Candidates must:

1. Attain three years of industry work experience.

2. Pass nine courses of instruction (seven core and two elective) within five years.

3. Complete 30 hours of continuing education every two years thereafter.

The ChFC course material is excellent and closely resembles the CFP® certification modules. Because of the excellent American College curriculum, ChFCs generally have an adequate amount of knowledge for providing financial advice.

USE AN INVESTMENT ADVISOR REPRESENTATIVE, NOT A SALESPERSON

In my world, there are two hats advisors wear: the Investment Advisor Representative (IAR) hat and the Registered Representative hat. As a consumer, you will rarely hear or see the Registered Rep title; rather, Registered Reps prefer to call themselves "advisors." I know that's confusing, but for whatever reason, industry regulators continue to allow Registered Reps to pretend like there are no distinctions. But there are; believe me.

Investment Advisor Representatives provide advice. Registered Reps provide products. That's the difference. These days, those in the industry who get a kick out of running financial plans and providing investment advice (like me) can do so without the confines and constrictions of a large Wall Street firm or insurance company "encouraging" us to sell their products.

I don't know why anybody, if given the choice, would choose to work with an advisor who is selling them products for their firm over an advisor who is providing advice. But the stodgy old ways of doing business die hard, mainly because they are still, even after so much disruption, insanely profitable to these firms. Why change anything if you can still make money hand over fist?

BEWARE OF HAT SWITCHERS

Registered Representatives and insurance agents sell their products using a consultative approach that makes it very difficult to distinguish from the real, actual, unbiased advice of modern-day Investment Advisor Representatives. Also, since there is little to no regulation regarding what Registered Representatives and insurance agents call themselves, it's difficult for the average consumer to make a distinction.

But get this: a Registered Representative and an Investment Advisor Representative *can be the same person.* This makes it nearly impossible to make a distinction unless, of course, you read this book. Amazingly, the regulators allow large financial services firms, like Merrill Lynch, UBS, Ameriprise, Edward Jones, and LPL, to employ salespeople who can be registered both ways, as Registered Representatives *and* Investment Advisory Representatives.

Let's call them hat switchers because the regulations allow representatives to take off their salesperson hat and provide advice for a fee, say in a managed account, then remove their advice hat and sell a lucrative, high-commission product for the firm. They can switch between hats at any time, multiple times, and even in the same meeting, all without the client knowing.

THE TROUBLE WITH HAT SWITCHERS

Do you think this sounds conflicted? If so, you're not alone. In recent years there has been a huge wave of money movement from these firms to smaller, stand-alone RIA firms. But as more and more money and clients move away from the large financial services firms, their salespeople follow.

A few make the move for the right reasons and drop their commission licenses in order to provide unbiased fee-only advice. However, most are maintaining their securities and insurance licenses in low-key arrangements. Beware; this advisor is the same conflicted hat switcher he was when employed at Ameriprise or LPL: a wolf in sheep's clothing. When evaluating advisor relationships, here are a few key questions to ask:

- **Are you affiliated with a broker/dealer or brokerage firm?** *Any* affiliation is a no-go, no matter how persuasive their answers may be. The name of their company may be something like XYZ Wealth, which could be a Registered Investment Advisory Firm where only advice and no product sales can occur. But you turn their card over or look at the fine print at the bottom of their website, and it will say something like, "Securities offered through ABC Financial, Member FINRA/SIPC. Investment advice offered through XYZ Financial, a registered investment advisor and separate entity from LPL Financial." If you see this, move on. The key words to avoid are "broker/dealer" and "FINRA."

- **How are you compensated?** Registered investment advisors are paid by the client, so this is the answer you are looking for. It could be a percentage of assets managed, a retainer, or a planning fee. The bottom line is that you pay it. Any answer like, "I get paid three ways," "It should not be a concern," or some other mumbo jumbo is unacceptable.

- **Do commissions make up any part of your compensation?** The answer should be "no." Many RIAs maintain an insurance license even if they don't have an affiliation with a broker/dealer for the sale of securities. Ask specifically about insurance commissions they may receive in relation to the recommendations they are providing.

It's important to note that some consumers believe they are getting unbiased advice when working with a discount brokerage firm like Schwab or Fidelity. Well, think again. These firms are providing transactional support for the buying and selling of securities and other financial products. Therefore, if or when they provide advice, it should *not* be considered unbiased or free from conflict. If you are relying on recommendations from your discount brokerage firm, understand there could be profit motives behind what they recommend.

There Is a Permanent Record, and It's Public

You may not know it, but yes, everyone in my industry has a record. And it can be easily verified a few ways. Remember, if you choose an advisor now, they could be with you for 30 years or more as you work toward and complete your long-term financial goals. Take the time to check out his or her service record.

A great way to check an advisor's record is through FINRA's BrokerCheck website. Go to https://brokercheck.finra.org and type in the advisor's name. Once you find him or her, here is what you are looking for:

- **PR – Previously Registered:** This means the advisor at one time held a securities license but is no longer registered. That's a good thing.

- **B – Broker:** This means the advisor currently holds a securities license of some type. As we discussed previously, this is not what you are looking for. Move on.

- **IA – Investment Advisor:** This means this advisor is an Investment Advisor Representative. Perfect!

Next there is a disclosures section. Disclosures are bad, so ideally the advisor you're looking into won't have any. But sometimes bad things happen to good advisors, so if there are disclosures, read them carefully and ask the advisor about them to better determine the circumstances.

Finally, there is an experience section where you can verify the advisor's work history and years of experience. Generally, of course, you are looking for a bigger number for years of experience and a smaller number for firms your advisor has worked for. An advisor who has bounced around a lot can mean a number of things, so you want to ask questions if you see a lot of firms listed.

From there, you can click over to www.adviserinfo.sec.gov and check out your investment advisor on the SEC website. This is where more information on RIAs and their representatives can be found. Most of the representative information is the same, but on the SEC website, you can get more detailed firm information. Search by your advisor's firm name and click on "Part 2 Brochures." This is the RIA firm's ADV Part II, and it has some fantastic information. Here you will find any disclosed conflicts of interest and verify the dollar amount of assets the firm manages, as well as their types of clients, number of accounts, fee schedules, and on and on.

It should take you all of about 15 minutes to quickly review the FINRA BrokerCheck and SEC Investment Adviser Public Disclosure sites for any red flags. If you see something that concerns you or that you don't understand, don't hesitate to take it up with the advisor. If, when you ask questions, the advisor becomes defensive, that's a bad sign. A good advisor will welcome your questions and concerns and should go out of their way to help you better understand their background and experience.

A Note About NAPFA

NAPFA stands for the National Association of Personal Financial Advisors, and their website is hands down the best place to find a truly independent, fee-only fiduciary advisor, which is exactly what you should be looking for.

Why? Because NAPFA is the exclusive association of these rare cats. To put this in context, let's throw in some numbers. There are approximately 300,000 investment advisors in the United States. Of those, about 80,000 are CFP® certificants, the most recognized distinction of profession expertise, as we discussed. Of those 80,000 CFP® certificants, less than 3,000 are willing to operate under the strict requirements and criteria of NAPFA.

That's because NAPFA takes it to the next level. To become a full member of NAPFA, you have to first be a CFP® certificant, and you must submit a comprehensive financial plan that you personally developed for peer review. Then, you have to meet NAPFA's strict criteria and definition as a fee-only advisor. This means you are disallowed from selling any financial products, including life insurance, for a commission. In addition, you cannot receive any referral fees from commission agents, or have any ownership in any financial services or insurance company or agency that sells commission products. You can easily use their website to search for a NAPFA member near you, and if I did my math correctly from the numbers of advisors illustrated above, you just eliminated 99% of the advisors out there in one fell swoop.

WHERE AND HOW ADVISORS GET PAID

Believe it or not, you'll have to pay good money for good financial advice. You get what you pay for. However, you should know how much it costs you and where the money comes from, so you can evaluate whether the advice you're getting is worth it. We already know the cost of not having any advice at all. It could cost you everything if you end up lost at sea, with no guidance on how to get where you need to go financially. But not all advisors charge the same rate or the same way, so their cost can be difficult to evaluate.

Here are some very general guidelines of what to reasonably expect with regard to your advisor's compensation:

- **AUM Fee:** AUM means "assets under management" in my world. In English, this is the amount of money your advisor is managing for you. It is most common for you to be charged a percentage on these assets as compensation for your advisor and his or her firm. Generally, most people should expect this fee to be around 1%, meaning if your assets at the firm are around one million dollars, you should expect to be charged around $10,000 per year. It can be more or less, depending on the size of your portfolio and/or the services being provided. In my opinion, for 1% of one million dollars, you should be getting a full wealth management experience that includes not only investment management but also comprehensive financial planning. Under no circumstances should an AUM fee exceed 1.5% of assets.

- **Financial Planning Fee:** An advisor may want to charge for all of the upfront preparations and time needed to create an initial financial plan. If so, this could be a one-time fee that pays for all of the upfront work associated with creating an initial comprehensive financial plan. This charge is going to vary widely, based upon the complexity of your situation and the comprehensiveness of the plan. The fee could possibly be as low as $500 for a young couple but could also exceed $80,000 for an extremely wealthy family with complex estate and tax planning issues. In my opinion, a reasonable planning fee for an average family should run between $3,000 and $8,000.

- **Retainer or Ongoing Planning Fee:** Instead of charging upfront or on assets, an advisor may charge a retainer or ongoing fee for as long as the engagement lasts. This could be a monthly charge or done on any preferred schedule. Just like the one-time planning fee, it could vary widely based upon the scope of work. Generally, this is a good way to go if all you want is ongoing financial planning advice without asset management.

- **Combo:** In today's environment, expect to see combinations of the three fee options used in conjunction with each other. For example: an advisor may charge only 40 basis points (0.4%) on assets managed but also a $3,000 semi-annual financial planning fee. On a $1 million portfolio, that's still 1% of assets, but charged differently. This is fine and can work to your advantage because it separates out the two services being provided a little (investment management and financial planning). However, make sure that you can add it all up and that it still makes sense, as a total charge, with respect to the services you are being provided.

THE WRONG WAY TO PAY AN ADVISOR

Nearly everybody in the financial services industry, regardless of how they get paid or what they call themselves, provides service in the way of consultative advice and assistance. This consultative sales technique looks, sounds, and feels like advice. Many times, it's useful and relevant, but at other times, it can be manipulative and detrimental to a client's long-term plan.

How do you tell the difference between good advice and bad advice? Well, you probably can't. The best salespeople in my industry are *that* good. They are extremely personable and likeable, so you will trust what they say. The stakes, in the form of commissions, are beyond lucrative in many cases. They have the opportunity to make upwards of $100,000 on a single transaction, payable up front at the time of sale. Stakes at this level create very, very good salespeople and can, unfortunately, encourage unscrupulous behavior. There are more than a few otherwise good people who will do or say the wrong thing for this kind of money.

Let's say you have a million dollars to invest. A commission-based advisor can sell you a loaded mutual fund and get paid around $10,000 on the transaction or write a variable annuity and make $60,000 or more on the transaction. The variable annuity will be the right choice in very few instances, mainly due to the high cost. But more often than you might believe, they sell the annuity. Go figure. And if you think you're smart enough to figure all of this out on your own, think again. Some of the most intelligent people I know have walked into my office with some of the absolute worst commission investment products in their portfolios. Remember, these salespeople are highly motivated and very good at what they do, so you won't see it coming.

Your golfing buddy who works for Merrill Lynch, Northwestern Mutual, or [insert financial services firm name here] is probably a nice guy and extremely successful. It's tempting, but you should not under any circumstances hire him to provide financial advice. He may be a good insurance agent or stock trader, but his advice is conflicted. Many times, we may need an insurance agent or stockbroker to assist us in purchasing financial products. But you should rely on a fee-only advisor to provide advice, make recommendations, and help you navigate toward your intended destination.

There is way too much at stake to rely on conflicted advice. We have to be ready and prepared at all times for whatever life throws at us, as illustrated in the next chapter.

Chapter 6

FUNERALS AND FIASCOS: PLANNING FOR WHAT CAN GO WRONG

It was a lazy Sunday afternoon when the tragic news reached me. I was drying off to lay back down in my lounge chair at the club. The kids were still in the water, splashing around, throwing the tennis ball at each other under the clear, blue, hot Texas summer sky. Back then, news still traveled here and there by word of mouth. One of our good friends, and a client, had been struck and killed by a drunk driver that morning. She was 39 years old. An avid triathlete, Meredith had been out riding with her training partner. The police later said there was no evidence the driver ever touched his brakes as his truck barreled into the bikes from behind, killing both riders instantly.

Sitting there on the edge of my chair, stunned, I watched my kids as they continued to play, splash, and laugh in the water. They were the same ages as Meredith and Sherman's three boys, the youngest being only six years old at the time. Tears flooded my eyes as a massive wave of emotion came over me.

Our entire community grieved. Everyone wanted to do something, to help in any way they could. But it's a helpless feeling, watching a family go through such a tough ordeal. As things started to settle down, Sherman and I got the opportunity to sit down and talk about things from a financial standpoint.

Fortunately, there was an adequate amount of life insurance, and their agent did a great job processing the claims quickly and efficiently. Sherman had a challenging and successful career with a solid, large company that provided him with the time off he desperately needed to take care of his boys. Eventually, he decided not to return to work. Instead, he took over the school his wife ran before her death. I respected Sherman for making such a selfless decision. His job required too much travel, and he was either going to have to run the school or sell it. We mapped out a plan where he would return to his career once the kids were a little older, but those plans morphed into other goals as time went on.

We invested much of the life insurance proceeds very conservatively at first. It was 2008, and we were unsure what expenses could present themselves over the next few years. So we wanted to be ready. Over the years, Sherman's business grew as he expanded their initial school into two, then three locations. Owning a local franchise business like the schools, he was able to maintain flexible hours and be available for the boys as a single parent. Sherman didn't remarry until much later. But today, he and his wife Jamie have moved into a beautiful new home and are building a new business franchise together. The boys are almost grown now and doing great. Looking back, I can say Sherman did a great job dealing with a tragic situation and making the best of it. I think there are three key takeaways here:

1. **Be prepared:** The life insurance Sherman and Meredith purchased provided critical options and a safety net for the family after Meredith's death.

2. **Sacrifice:** When tragedy strikes your family, someone will be making tough decisions. If you make the right decisions for the right reasons, it usually works out in the end.

3. **Plan:** Because he had to sacrifice, Sherman found himself in a job he didn't necessarily want, but he made

the best of it. He stayed motivated and found success by planning ahead. He had a financial endgame in his sights the whole time. Now, 12 years later, he's living it.

As you craft your finances, sometimes you have to take off your optimist hat and think about the bad things that could happen. When I was in the Navy, we had to train around worst case scenarios to make sure nobody got killed. That's why, when I talk about things going wrong, I refer to it as a lifeboat drill.

Successful personal financial planning and maturity go hand in hand. In a lifeboat drill, we come up with different scenarios, emergencies, and tragedies that could happen, and we talk through what needs to be done in those situations. When the unexpected comes and whacks us smack in the face, we need to be ready.

DEATH

Death can be sudden and absolutely shocking, as was the case when Meredith was killed. Have you ever had a brush with death? I have. (I'll explain later.) Have you ever thought about it from a financial standpoint? What expenses would be associated with your death? How would your family continue on financially without you? Every day, people die in the prime of their lives, and it can have a massive financial impact upon their families.

Life insurance was invented to provide funds to your family in case of death, and it's relatively inexpensive. But it's got to be one of the most frustrating financial products on Earth. Why? Because the right information you need in order to make a good buying decision rarely ever presents itself. There is a whole industry out there vying for your premium dollar with conflicting information and opinions that will make your head spin.

Driving down the road on Saturday morning listening to talk radio, you'll hear financial gurus railing against traditional life insurance as a complete rip-off. "Buy term and invest the rest," they'll say. Then after a brief pause, "And now, a word from our sponsor, Zander Insurance, where *you* should buy your term insurance!" Hmmm.

Later, you're playing golf at the club, and a fellow member who works for Northwestern Mutual Life argues, "No. Buying term is like renting. You want to *own* your coverage, so it will be there when you die." Makes sense, but you wonder how much of your premium is paying for his new PXG irons.

Life Insurance: The Easy Way

So, which is better? It depends on your situation. If you knew when you were going to die, you could back into the numbers and definitely come up with a fantastic decision. But you're not holding those cards, so let's explore further.

There are basically three types of life insurance: term, universal life, and whole life. Variants exist with different nuances, names, and features, but they all fit within one of these three categories.

Term: The Brainless Option

If you're in a hurry to get life insurance until you figure out your entire financial plan, and you should be, term insurance is for you. You can get term insurance quickly by calling an insurance broker or jumping on the internet. It doesn't cost a lot, and you're covered until you figure everything out.

Term insurance is by far your least expensive option. You can buy a large amount of coverage for a very small premium amount. But there's a catch, and the catch is that it's only going to be in place for a certain amount of time, or a term (hence the name). Generally, these days we buy term insurance in increments of ten years. So, you would buy a 10-year level term, a 20-year, or maybe even a 30-year level term product.

What happens after the term expires? Well, the insurance company will usually continue to offer coverage but at an astronomical price. I have a client whose 10-year term just expired, and his annual premium is going from $6,200 to $68,000 for $1 million in coverage. Ouch! If he wants to continue to have coverage, he has two other options:

1. He can go out into the marketplace and buy a new 10-year term insurance policy. But he'll have to prove he is healthy, otherwise he may not be able to purchase another policy.

2. If one is available with his carrier, he can convert his term policy into a different type of policy. This will be expensive but possibly better than just paying the 11th year term cost at $68,000.

That's the problem with term insurance: it's going to come to an end. More often than not, I'd say my clients who buy term insurance are *not* really ever ready for their term to expire. Usually that's okay; you can go out and buy another term policy for another 10 years or so. But sometimes health conditions creep in that create a problem. If you still need the coverage but can't get it, this can leave your family exposed.

WHOLE LIFE: THE EXPENSIVE OPTION

At the other end of the spectrum is whole life. Whole life is defined by a guaranteed level premium with a cash value component that endows at age 100. What does that mean? It means, the insurance company is going to guarantee that your premium will never change, ever, and that your coverage will stay in force for the rest of your life. Simple. If you reach age 100, the endowment of a $100,000 policy means you have $100,000 of cash built up inside the policy, equaling the death benefit, and you're done, endowed.

Cash builds up in a whole life policy over time and is credited with a dividend at a modest guaranteed rate, kind of like a CD or bond. You either get the cash or the death benefit but not both. One effective way to use the cash is to loan yourself money from your policy, then pay it back. I have a policy, where I can loan myself money at a current rate of 5%. It's collateralized by the cash buildup in my policy, which is making 3.2%. This means my cost of funds is only 1.8%, well below any other loan source rate available to me. This is an example of a living benefit that is not available on term policies. But be aware, using a policy in this way is an advanced planning situation with lots of complexity. Even though it's a loan to yourself, it's still a loan and can have negative consequences if not managed properly.

If you pay one premium and croak, the return on investment (for your family, not you) is astounding. More importantly, as mentioned before, the money is coming in right when your family needs it most. If, on the other hand, you live a long, full life, the return on investment or premium when you die is not nearly as high, but still very likely to be positive. It's definitely not as high of a return as you could have made in a diversified investment portfolio, but in the likely case you outlive a term policy, the "return" is - zero, right?

Sounds great? Hold on. The catch is that the premium for whole life insurance is astoundingly high compared to term insurance premiums, as in sometimes 10 times as expensive. That's so high, few if any young families who need life insurance the most can afford the premium for the coverage they need. It makes sense that the premium would be higher because the benefits and guarantees are much higher, but we're talking astoundingly high. There's an old saying that life insurance is sold, not bought. That Northwestern Agent with the PXG irons? He gets paid a very nice commission on the products he sells. How much? Who really knows? Whole life policies are what we call a "bundled" product. This means you won't find any information on costs within the policy, so it's impossible to know what the policy is really costing you.

The other problem with whole life is its inflexibility. Generally, just like term, the premium and the death benefit are fixed and cannot be adjusted. So if your circumstances change, it's hard to adjust your policy to keep up with what is going on in your life.

Universal Life: The Flexible Option

The third and final product we will discuss is universal life insurance. Universal life, or UL, can be called all sorts of things and has many different components, so we'll just go over the basics that you need to know.

Think of UL has a hybrid between whole life and term. UL always has a cash value component, just like whole life, but instead of dividends, the policy earns interest. Variable universal life, a variant of UL, even has an investment component that allows you to take investment return risk and reap investment return earnings.

But unlike whole life, it generally does not have strong guarantees regarding level lifetime premiums or endowment of the cash value. Instead, UL provides a great deal of flexibility in both premiums and sometimes death benefits that you don't get with whole life or term.

Finally, UL provides better transparency. You can see all of the costs, like the actual cost of insurance, fees, taxes, and investment expenses, all lined out year by year. This, I believe, makes UL a more competitive product than whole life. With a little research, you can shop for the best carrier with the best price.

But it's the flexibility that makes UL so appealing to me. You can buy a UL policy and pay near term premium payments, and it will act a lot like a term product. Or, you can overfund your UL, and it will accumulate cash and last a lifetime, just like whole life. Or mix it up, like I have done.

When my family was young and I needed a lot of coverage, I bought a large death benefit and paid the lowest premium allowed. As I started making more money, I increased the amount I was paying in premiums to strengthen the policy a little. In recent years, I let the term insurance I also had expire, but I continued to fund my variable UL at very strong premium levels. The cash accumulation is available to me if I want it at the 1.8% cost of funds previously mentioned. Or, I can fund my policy so heavily, that it stays in force through my retirement without any additional premiums after age 65.

The Big UL Mistake: Set and Forget

The biggest mistake most people make with UL is that they set it and forget it. When you first buy any life insurance policy, the agent will show you an illustration of what it's expected to do over the life of the policy. With term and whole life, you can expect your policy to do what the illustration shows. But because UL has so many variables, and fewer guarantees, you cannot rely on the initial illustration. If you own a UL policy, you should order an in-force illustration every year to see how your policy is performing and make adjustments as necessary. Think of UL as a living financial product, not a set-in-stone premium expense.

How Much Insurance Do You Need?

So that's life insurance 101, but you still cannot decide what type of coverage to buy until you know how much you need. I always tell families that the first place you go to determine how much coverage you need is to your own personal experience and instincts. A lot of times, you'll kind of know in the back of your mind what that amount should be. If you have a young family and are just starting out, start with your instincts and just buy some coverage *now*. You're young, term coverage will be inexpensive, and an untimely death would be catastrophic to your family, so don't delay.

Whew! So, your family is covered, now what? A life insurance analysis is probably in order. It's a good exercise to go thru for a couple of reasons: The analysis will provide peace of mind that your coverage is adequate. It also provides an opportunity to talk through the consequences of an untimely death, so you and your family are prepared for the worst.

Below is an example of a life insurance needs analysis (*larger image of worksheet available in the end chapter of book*) :

LIFE INSURANCE NEEDS ANALYSIS					
				John	Molly
Liquid Assets					
	Cash/Checking			$30,000	$30,000
	Savings			$14,000	$14,000
	Bonds				
	Life Insurance			$123,000	$157,000
	Term at Work				$120,000
		TOTAL		$137,000	$291,000
Liabilities (to be paid off if client dies today)					
	Mortgage (only if house is to be sold)		$0	$0
	Debts			$0	$0
	Final Medical Expenses			$17,500	$17,500
	Funeral Expenses			$8,000	$8,000
	Probate			$1,500	$1,500
	Estate Taxes			$0	$0
	Adjustment Fund			$9,800	$58,800
		TOTAL		$36,800	$85,800
	TOTAL IMMEDIATE NEED			-$100,200	-$205,200
PV of Income Needed with Children				$0	$210,966
Education				$120,000	$120,000
PV of Income Need during Blackout				$0	$290,325
PV of Income Need in Retirement				$0	$0
Emergency Fund					
	TOTAL FINANCIAL NEED			$120,000	$621,291
	TOTAL LIFE INSURANCE NEED			$19,800	$416,091

Let's walk through this analysis, which tries to take into account any immediate needs, along with any future needs for your family in case you die. In the first section called "Liquid Assets," we add up all of the readily accessible money that is available in case of death for John and then for Molly. As you can see, we include checking accounts, savings accounts, and any life insurance that would pay out on the other spouse's death.

Next, we add up all of the potential liabilities. This includes any current debt, usually the mortgage, maybe a car payment, possible medical expenses associated with final expenses, funeral costs, attorney fees, and then something called an "adjustment fund." The adjustment fund allows the surviving spouse some time away from work to make arrangements and deal with the tragic transition that follows the death of a loved one. In Sherman's case, his employer was extremely benevolent and provided him with paid time off. This is not always the case, so you may want to plan on having money available for this need.

From there it gets a little complicated. But hang with me, and I think I can explain the general concept. In life insurance planning, we divide the surviving spouse's life into three phases: Phase 1 is with kids in the home; Phase 2 is after the kids leave but before retirement, called the "Blackout Phase;" and Phase 3 is retirement. We use these phases because of Social Security.

Did you know Social Security pays surviving widows or widowers and school-age children a monthly benefit? Most people don't know this. You can find this benefit on your Social Security annual statement, and you'll probably be surprised how much it is. For John, Molly, and their kids in this illustration, it's $5,100 per month. That amount is sufficient for John, along with his income, to be fine without any additional funds during this period. For Molly, a time value calculation solves for a $211,000 present value lump sum needed to provide additional monthly income during Phase 1. You can also see that education needs for the kids are also calculated in there. Sometimes it's tough to save for college as a single parent.

In Phase 2, the Blackout Phase, there is no Social Security provided. In this scenario, the time value calculation came up with another $290,000 in present value funds needed to provide monthly income to Molly during this phase.

In Phase 3, the Retirement Phase, Social Security comes back into the picture. Widows and widowers are allowed to draw a reduced amount of Social Security early, at age 60, if they desire. John and Molly don't need additional funds because they have adequate retirement funds in place.

At the end of the spreadsheet, everything is summed up. All of the available cash and life insurance proceeds minus immediate and future needs. Now we have a good idea how much life insurance is needed, but more importantly, we have a plan. Just going through the exercise allows families to think through a tragic loss, talk about the options and decisions, and formulate a plan, just in case. That's why we call it a lifeboat drill.

THE TEST

Several years ago, on a Friday morning, I discovered a lump deep in the tissue toward the back of my tongue. My buddy Dr. Michael Sheppard, an oral surgeon, worked me in that morning to check it out. He was perplexed and concerned enough to pull some strings and get me in with Dr. Yadro Ducic, a top head and neck cancer surgeon that very afternoon. Dr. Ducic took a look and said, "I don't know what that is, but we need to get it out of your mouth and into a bucket." He scheduled me for surgery the following week.

That weekend, I was left to ponder the very clear and present reality that I might have cancer, and that it could kill me. Amazingly, I wasn't scared. I adamantly believe that, once this life is over, there is another dimension where I will know my Creator. Also,

I knew with 100% certainty that my family would be fine from a financial standpoint because of the insurance coverage on my life. This knowledge took a *huge* load off my shoulders when I needed it the most.

Fortunately, Dr. Ducic was able to remove the tumor, and it turned out to be benign. The moral of the story is that we will all be tested at some point. We never know when, so plan ahead so that you don't end up worrying about things you have no control over.

DISABILITY

Believe it or not, you're much more likely to become disabled at some point during your working career than die. Yet, I would say only a fraction of the people who own life insurance also have disability insurance. You should seriously consider disability coverage. If you are not able to work, either permanently or for an extended period of time, both you and your family are going to suffer financially. If you have disability coverage, the insurance company will step in after a period of time and pay a partial percentage of what you were making in your job.

Disability insurance is a complicated product, with all kinds of unfamiliar terms, tax considerations, and iterations. You'll need more than this brief sub-chapter to make an informed decision. I strongly recommend that you seek professional guidance from a financial planner or insurance agent when purchasing disability income insurance.

Typical disability income policies work like this. Let's say you have a stroke. Usually, you'll continue to get paid for a little while by your employer as sick leave, but after that's exhausted, they can't pay you even if they want to. In order for a company to deduct your pay as a company expense, you have to work for it. So, after a while, if you're not working, they're not paying. If you have short-term disability insurance through your employer, it will probably start to pay you a weekly benefit as soon as you file the claim, or maybe after a week or so, but it will stop at some point, usually after 90 days.

In my opinion, short-term disability is great if your company is paying for it but not so great if you are paying for it. If you're following my advice and maintaining good, solid cash reserves at all times, you don't need short-term disability because you have cash ready to deploy. That's called self-insuring, and it works great for manageable risk, like being out of work for a couple of months.

But after 90 days or so, things could get a little hairy as that next mortgage payment looms large over a rapidly diminishing savings account. This is generally right when a long-term disability income policy kicks in and saves the day. The first 90 days are called the elimination period. (It can be 30, 60, 90, or 180 days, but it's usually 90 days.) This means you have to wait 90 days before the insurance company starts paying a claim. This does *not* mean you wait 90 days before *filing* a claim. You want to file your claim as soon as possible in order to make sure your payments start on time.

Once started, the payments will continue until either you are able to go back to work or until the policy benefit period ends. The benefit period comes in a few flavors too. Two years, five years, or to age 65 are the most common benefit periods. The longer the benefit period, the more expensive the premium. Choose what you want, but I usually recommend a benefit period of up to age 65 because a permanent disability would be traumatic and hard to handle financially otherwise.

The benefit amount is usually 60% of your pre-disability earnings up to a maximum monthly amount. "Why not 100%?" you might ask. The answer is insurance fraud. Apparently, there are people out there who would rather not work and get paid the same regardless. At 60%, you should still be able to make the mortgage payment and handle basic expenses, but you'll be motivated to rehabilitate and return to work.

Did you know that Social Security pays disability income benefits? Yup. Don't get your hopes up because it's hard to qualify, but there's a trick. Most insurance companies provide an optional provision on their policies called Social Security Integration. If you accept it, they discount the premium by a decent amount. If you have integration and you go on claim, your carrier will work aggressively on your behalf to file for Social Security Disability Income (SSDI). If it pays, they then reduce your monthly benefit by the amount paid, so your total payment between Social Security and your insurance carrier remains the same at 60% of pre-disability earnings. This is nice because the insurance company assists with all of the bureaucratic red tape, you get the same amount regardless of the outcome, it saves you premium dollars, and if your disability lasts for two years, you're now eligible for Medicare.

Confusing Definitions

When it comes to insurance, it's all about definitions, and nowhere is that more true than disability income policies. Here is what to watch for:

- **Residual vs. Total Disability:** If given the option, you want a policy that pays for partial disability because it's an easier hurdle. Let's say your stroke rehabilitation has gone great, and the doctor says you can go back to work on a part-time basis, no more than four hours per day. Under a total disability definition, your claim checks stop, but under a partial disability definition, you could still get 60% of the difference between what you made full time before and what you are making part time now.

- **Own Occupation vs Any Occupation:** If you can get it, you want own occupation coverage because this means that if you cannot return to the job or career you had previously, the insurance company will still pay your benefit. Any occupation means that if you are not qualified to conduct brain surgery like you were before the stroke but you can work as a Walmart greeter, they can potentially take you off claim.

DON'T ACCIDENTALLY BUY ACCIDENT INSURANCE

I see people get tricked by this all of the time, so don't fall for it. At the insurance company, they have actuarial data that can give them a real edge when it comes to risk assessment. As humans, when we think of disability, we think of a car accident or some other accidental injury. But most disabilities are not from accidents. Rather, they are from cancer, stroke, heart failure, kidney failure, diabetes, ALS, Parkinson's, and so forth. Accident policies are cheap but generally not worth the money. To be adequately protected, you need coverage regardless of how the disability occurred.

That goes for life insurance too. AD&D, or accidental death and dismemberment, is a very common offering, either stand alone or as a rider. If you want to buy it, that's fine, but it's not an alternative to true life or disability coverage. The same holds true for accident and sickness policies, cancer policies, or dread disease policies. The common thread of all of these coverages is that they lay out very specific criteria your circumstance must meet in order to make a claim. Real life insurance and disability coverage does not spell out specific criteria. Their definitions are more broad in nature.

UMBRELLA LIABILITY COVERAGE

As you become more financially successful, you start to have more to lose, and unfortunately others may see your success as an opportunity for themselves. Anybody can get sued for anything, regardless of fault or actions. The best way to protect yourself is to have umbrella liability coverage. An umbrella policy is well named because it means no matter where you or your family are, either at home, in your car, someone else's car, or just walking down the street, you're covered. Over the years, I've seen clients get sued for all sorts of things from jet ski accidents to elevator malfunctions. These days, the bottom line is, if somebody gets hurt, there is probably going to be a lawsuit. Cover yourself with an umbrella policy. It's usually fairly inexpensive and comes in $1-million-dollar increments. If you get sued, the insurance company will provide your defense and pay any settlement or judgement up to policy limits.

LONG-TERM CARE

When we plan out a retirement for a client, we try to load it up with any and all contingencies that are likely to come up. When we throw the graph up on the screen of asset accumulation, then decumulation over the course of the client's retirement period, toward the end, many times it takes a big nosedive. "What's that?" the client invariably asks in a higher than normal, concerned tone. "That's long-term care," I say. Then we talk about it.

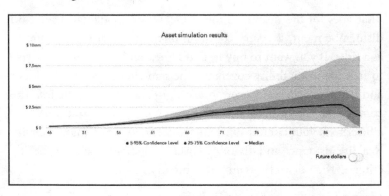

Long term care is becoming a real challenge in the world of financial planning. If you don't know what it is, long-term care is the professional and non-professional care needed when somebody is unable to perform regular activities of daily living on their own. Assistance can be provided in a number of ways and locations, either at home or in a nursing facility. And it can be provided by professional medical staff, like occupational therapists, or by non-professional caregivers. The cost of this assistance keeps going up at three times the rate of normal CPI inflation. It's hard to put a number on what it costs because it depends on the care needed, but we assume a minimum of $48,000 a year in our estimates, in today's dollars. It's also hard to know how long you might need it or when.

Because of the cost and uncertainty, this contingency becomes a moderately good candidate for shifting the risk to an insurance company in the form of a long-term care insurance policy. The problem is, it's so likely to happen, the insurance company has to charge significantly high premiums for the coverage.

Should you buy long-term care insurance? I think it depends. When we run our retirement plans, if our assumptions of cost look more like a blip and less like a nosedive, we will many times recommend that a client self-insure for long-term care costs. What this means is, they have adequate assets to cover the cost and then some, so they are not in danger of running out of money.

If the plan nosedives, that means the cost of long-term care is too great for their projected asset balances later in life. We'll normally encourage them to seek out a quote for long-term care insurance with a good independent insurance agent. From there, we can input the proposal assumptions and see if their plan runs a little better. If their ongoing cash flow can handle the premiums, and if the coverage pulls the nosedive of the plan up to a manageable level, then we'll recommend they purchase a policy.

To keep the premiums down, we usually recommend at least a 90-day elimination period. Besides, many times Medicare will pay much of the cost of long-term care up to 100 days. The longest benefit period you can get is 5 years, and that's what we recommend. I wish there was a product that had a really long elimination period, like two years, then an unlimited benefit period, but the insurance companies won't bite on that, unfortunately.

To go on claim, it's pretty much the same criteria for all qualified long-term care plans. There are six activities of daily living (ADLs) and then what I call the trump card. The six ADLs are eating, bathing, getting dressed, toileting, transferring, and continence. If your doctor certifies that you have lost the ability to perform two or more of these ADLs, then your insurance company should put you on claim. The trump card is cognitive ability. If you lose cognitive ability through Alzheimer's, dementia, or any other cause, that in and of itself meets the criteria for going on claim.

Most policies in force these days pay claims on a reimbursement basis. That means, you have to pay for care, then submit to the carrier for reimbursement. You also need to be careful and make sure your care provider is approved with your carrier. Careful co-ordination with your insurance carrier will ensure that your claims are processed smoothly. It's not an enjoyable process, but they all seem to be like that. You can purchase coverage for professional care only or just for skilled nursing facilities, but I recommend professional and non-professional, along with in-home coverage, so you can keep your options open.

Because of the high inflation risk, there are inflation riders you can purchase as part of your policy. These riders are very confusing and sometimes very expensive. Due to the cost variations, you will have to evaluate them for yourself, but I have a good tip that might work. Many times, you can purchase a much higher benefit amount, even double, for less than the top-level compound inflation rider. So why not just buy the extra coverage now? That can work well.

Finally, here is the real bummer with long-term care insurance. You think it's expensive now? Just wait because the premium is not guaranteed. Just like your home, auto, or medical insurance, your premium can go up. I say "can" go up, but you might as well expect it to go up. So when, or if, you buy it, keep this in mind.

Taking off our optimist hat every once in a while is an important part of planning for our future. We know everything is not going to be unicorns and rainbows, so putting in the work to evaluate different risks will pay off. Many of the things that can go wrong can be smartly and efficiently covered with insurance. For others, awareness and a contingency plan may be all we can do or all we really even need. Okay, now put your optimist hat back on before anybody sees you.

Chapter 7

THE HARDEST EASY

I enjoy duck hunting. I know that there must be something seriously wrong with me, but I love it mainly because of the challenge. You may think, "Challenge? Shooting such a large bird while it slowly lands on the water should be easy." And you would be correct if that was all there was to it. Hunters like to call duck hunting the hardest easy hunting there is, just like I call retirement investing the hardest easy investing there is.

Let me take you through a recent duck hunt my son and I experienced, and you will see what I mean. The night before, I went and picked up my boat and carefully packed all of our gear in the truck, including decoys, guns, ammo, dog crate, chest waders, coats, chairs, portable blind, and all. Just a few short hours later, I woke Daniel up at 2 a.m., and we drove three hours to a small lake near Abilene. Daniel was dead asleep when I turned a little too early and ended up on a mud road, but he was awake with a start as I redlined my truck to get through a soggy washout. We barely made it.

At the boat ramp we found competition, another group of duck hunters. We hurriedly scrambled to see who would launch first and get dibs on the best spot. The other hunters won, but at least our motor started in the freezing cold. We ran down the lake in the dark, fortunately didn't hit anything, and got to our spot in plenty of time. I jumped out of the boat, took three steps, and found a sharp stump with my shin. Within seconds, freezing lake water had filled my left wader boot.

As I retreated to land, Daniel started setting out decoys. I set up the blind and started carrying gear from the boat to the blind. Guns, where were the guns? ...In the truck. In our rush to get launched, we forgot a key piece of equipment. After another boat ride, Daniel, Beaux the black lab, and I were finally locked and loaded. We had several big groups of birds come by. But any time they looked interested, the other group of hunters would shoot, and they would spook. Finally, by mid-morning, things came together, and we were able to scratch down a few nice mallards.

See what I mean? Just like a duck hunt, when investing, sometimes we are our own worst enemy. The actions we take can end up hurting us more than they help us.

WE ARE OUR OWN WORST ENEMY... THEN THERE'S INFLATION

When investing, most of the things that go wrong have to do with ourselves, not the stock market. We're not investing because it's fun; we're investing because we have to. We are looking for long-term returns that will beat the inflation rate over the long haul. If we don't beat inflation, we probably are not going to be successful. That's serious pressure.

The financial crisis was a long time ago now, yet I still meet folks from time to time who went to cash during the downturn and are still in cash. It's heartbreaking because I know the severe negative impact this has on their retirement goals. The only saving grace has been the relatively low inflation we have experienced over the last few years. However, return on cash in savings or money market accounts has been next to nothing over that time, so we are still looking at around 20% erosion of purchasing power. Let's say a couple that was 50 years old in 2009 had a $500,000 investment portfolio that dropped 25% before they pulled the trigger and cashed out at $375,000 in January of 2009. With inflation, 10 years later they only have $300,000 in inflation-adjusted equivalent dollars that will continue to erode every single year they remain in cash.

On the flipside, let's say they held in there and stayed invested. The S&P 500 went on a tear for the 10 years after the crisis, up well over 200% from January 2009 to January 2019. Let's assume our 50-year-old couple did not possess a crystal ball, so they played it safe and smart, diversifying and spreading their money across asset classes. They kept almost half of their money out of the stock market entirely, investing 40% in bonds instead in order to maintain their sanity. A portfolio designed this way could have returned 8% or more on an annual return basis from 2009 to 2019. Compounded, their $375,000 in January 2009 would be topping $800,000 10 years later. Inflation still takes a 20% bite out of it over that 10-year period and leaves them with $640,000 in 2009 inflation-adjusted equivalent dollars.

$300,000 vs. $640,000 is obviously enough of a difference to make or break a couple's retirement plans. It takes courage to resist the fear market volatility creates in us. We have to remember this.

TAKING ON RISK TO INCREASE OUR CHANCES OF SUCCESS

At this point, you might be asking yourself, "Isn't there an easier way?" If my goal was to make a quick buck, I would enthusiastically say, "Yes! Just sign up for my workshop on [insert the latest infomercial topic] for guaranteed success!"

But I'm afraid there is no easier way; it's just not how this works. There is risk, and there is return. And they are joined at the hip. In order to make a return on our money over the inflation rate, we have to put our money at risk. How much risk? Really not *that* much, but enough risk to probably make us a little uncomfortable.

No person and no product out there can deliver a guaranteed return at any meaningful level above inflation. What you will find is the guarantee weakens as you move up the return scale. US government bonds are considered the safest investments on the planet so you will find their return to be somewhere around or even below the inflation rate. From there we move up into CDs, annuities, municipal bonds, investment grade corporate bonds, and high-yield debt. Generally speaking, the return will be in proportion to the risk or, rather, the value of the guarantee.

If somebody says a return is guaranteed, you should always ask, "By whom?" And keep asking questions until you reveal the true risks associated with the potential return. The risk is there; just sometimes you have to dig to find it.

CDs, bonds, and annuities can all play an important role in an investment portfolio because they do possess some level of guarantee. They generally help us at least keep up with inflation, so we don't go backwards. But their role is a supporting role, not one of a primary creator of real return over the inflation rate.

Real estate and other tangible assets can play an important role too. If you buy a piece of real estate as an investment, there is no guarantee of its future value, but at least you have something physical you can see and feel. A good real estate investment should beat inflation, but maybe not by as much as you would think or hope. Real estate investments also have carrying costs (insurance and taxes), and buildings decay over time requiring maintenance and renovation. These costs can significantly eat into returns, especially if costs increase with inflation over time and your rents remain stagnant.

Also, we must consider the marketability of real estate. Real estate is considered fairly illiquid because it could take a while to find a willing buyer of your property if you need to sell it, depending upon where we are in the market cycle. A good argument for real estate I hear often is that "they are not making any more of it." This is true, unless you take into account ocean reclamation or space colonization. If populations continue to grow, there will be more demand for more and more real estate so the laws of supply and demand should therefore dictate higher prices.

But what if we could find an investment that's not as constrained by the laws of supply and demand? You can, and it's called common stock. I know; now I'm sounding like that infomercial. But hear me out. Stock is by far the best investment to use as our primary driver of real return over the inflation rate.

What Is Stock? And Why Own It?

We tend to forget what stock is and what it represents. Billions of dollars of stocks are traded each day with continual fluctuations in prices at such a fast and furious pace it defies comprehension. For this reason, it's easy to lose sight of what we actually purchase when we buy publicly traded stocks. Simply put, the stocks we buy represent equity stakes in a business venture. That's it, plain and simple.

It's best if we forget the arbitrage aspect since our goal is long-term growth. This means about 99% of what you read, watch, or hear about the stock market each day has no relevance. If you don't believe me, turn on CNBC right now and try to pay attention. After 20 minutes, ask yourself, "Has anything I just watched provided me with any guidance I could use over a 10-year holding period?" Sure, you might catch somebody talking about a hot stock or when they think the economy is going to turn, but none of this is important over the long term (even if they are correct, which is usually a coin toss).

So, what *is* relevant? People, creative people. Believe what you want, but I believe we were created by a Creator and He created us to be creative, like Him. Whether this fits into your worldview or not doesn't matter; you can't deny that humans are constantly coming up with new ideas. We can't help ourselves. For example, I was carving wood decoys in my shop the other day, and my bench vise was not providing the freedom I wanted to carve different angles. I jumped on YouTube and found a carver in Oklahoma who had created a nifty carving vise using a trailer hitch ball. His invention touched my inner redneck. One thing led to another, and next thing I knew, I had created an improved prototype for my buddy Chuck Petrek to have his mechanical guys fabricate for me.

From computer chips to phones, to social media platforms, to driverless cars, to just about anything, this creative process continues to advance and accelerate. People imagine, plan, and build new stuff constantly using our species' unique creativity. Some of these people work in publicly traded companies, and when you own stock, you are participating financially in their creative process. Because of this creativity, companies where people work can increase in value at a much greater clip than other investments, like real estate and gold, the values of which are closely bound to scarcity or the laws of supply and demand.

This is why the growth rate of the stock market is often times compared to the increase in value over time of fine works of art. A talented artist creates something of great value out of nothing but canvas and oils, just like a semiconductor company creates the latest computer chip out of sand. Over the long run, other investments lag because they lack this creative component. The modern stock market allows any and all of us to participate in the potential return that creative and talented people can generate within publicly traded companies.

NOT GUARANTEED

So it's simple. We just have to pick out a few stocks we think are kind of cool and the rest is easy, right? Wrong. Information, pricing, and trading in the stock market move at a pace measured in milliseconds. The markets are built by and for the investment firms, high frequency traders, and arbitrage specialists who live, eat, and breathe this stuff every millisecond of every trading day. It's their pond. If we try to play their games, by their rules, in their pond, we lose.

The good news is, we don't have to play their games. We're just going to float above the water and ride the waves they make to long-term success. This means we should resist making any assumptions about any single company or particular stock. We want to be agnostic as to individual names or ticker symbols. Rather, we want to purchase baskets of stocks. This is called diversification, and it works. The more stocks, the better, and the less likely you are to fall prey to the industry machine.

We know overall creativity will generate return, but we don't know where or when. If we buy baskets of stocks, our baskets will float along and rise over time as the creativity of people like us, in various companies and industries, create value and profitability. In a fully diversified portfolio, we can reap the benefits of stock appreciation over time, as long as we can accept the volatility that comes with being invested in an extremely efficient marketplace. As long-term, diversified investors, we choose not to participate in the arbitrage and daily trading that occurs in order to reap the benefits of the market efficiencies they help create.

A WORD ABOUT VOLATILITY

We can successfully diversify away a lot of the risk and noise created around individual stocks in the stock market pond, but the waves of up and down momentum are something we definitely feel and must contend with. We must think long term because the frantic movements smooth out over days, weeks, months, and years into mountain graphs of long-term growth we can clearly see over historical periods of time.

But it's easier said than done. Maybe this conceptual illustration will help. It's not uncommon for any number of well-known stocks to trade 10 or 20 million times every day. Each trade represents a new consensus on the stock's value between a buyer and a seller, so that consensus happened 10 million or so times at various prices during the course of the trading day. Now imagine you put your house on the market this morning, and by 4 p.m. Eastern Standard Time, it had changed hands 10 *million times*. That's potentially 10 million people climbing in the attic, inspecting your sprinkler system, and running market analysis to determine value. Do you think by, say, the millionth transaction that just about every known defect and market factor affecting your home value had been uncovered? Surely.

Now let's say this crazy activity continued day after day, week after week, month after month, and year after year. We would then have to consider your home a marketable security, with extreme liquidity. It's still a home, but the price is being determined instantaneously throughout the day, based upon known changes and market factors.

My point is sometimes we assume an investment like a home to be safer than it really is just because its price does not appear to fluctuate. But the price *would* fluctuate if it had the same marketability as a stock in the stock market. To invest properly for long-term returns, we must allow all of this frantic trading to occur below the surface and try to ignore it as best we can. Later, much later, we'll be glad this liquidity exists because it allows us to easily convert our investments into income for retirement.

More Baskets, More Better

If we have one basket with lots of stocks in it, our investments are considered to be diversified, but that's not enough. The more stocks we have the better, but having more different types of stocks, bonds, or other types of investments is ideal. We want assorted baskets. When we have several baskets that span the spectrum of available investments, it's called asset allocation. Each of your baskets holds different types of stocks, bonds, real estate, coin collections, or whatever.

Anytime I stumble upon a new investment concept, philosophy, fund, etc. that I like, I build out a new basket. Will my new basket beat the market next year? Who knows? Who cares? That's not what I build it for. The new basket simply represents one more opportunity out of many, reduces my reliance on just one basket, and reduces the risk of my overall portfolio.

At the beginning of any investment year, it's fun to watch all of the experts predict how the different asset classes are going to perform. It rarely turns out the way they thought. There's very little predictability to any of it. So much so, a large number of professional investors like me don't pay any attention. Rather, we simply spread our risk across asset classes (or baskets). This reduces the risk of getting hammered too bad by one asset class underperforming and increases the chance that at least some of our invested money does well.

Going back to our pond illustration, imagine you are floating along, and all of these different investments are creating different waves. Some of the waves move in different directions or with different frequencies, but others line up in harmony. This creates a slightly smoother ride, especially when we add some non-stock asset classes like real estate and bonds.

However, we could broaden our horizons even further. The S&P 500 is the largest 500 publicly traded companies in the US, but there are actually over 4,000 publicly traded US companies available to investors. We should invest in as many of them as we can because it increases our probability of owning some great performers, while spreading our risk out even further.

We should not stop there. There are well over 8,000 publicly traded stocks available on major exchanges in Tokyo, Hong Kong, London, and elsewhere in the world. These stocks represent some of the greatest potential for return, especially in emerging markets where growth has at times been astounding.

If there is one thing we learned in 2008, it's that you can't over-diversify. The more stocks the better, with varied company size, industries, and countries of origin. You never know what industry, sector, or country is going to outperform, so spread out along as many lines as you can.

MARKET TIMING

I don't have much to say on the topic of market timing except don't fixate on it. Always remember a decision to come out of the market is only half of the equation. You may get it right, but now you have to figure out when to get back in. Market timers rarely win in the long term because the probability of getting in *and* getting out at the right time is low.

I know riding the market down goes against all common sense. As we watch our portfolio shrivel, fear and instincts kick in and start screaming at us, "Sell, stupid, before there is nothing left!" But that same fear and instinct will not allow us to invest back in because the buying signals are never clear enough to overcome our human fear of loss. So, there we are, stuck in cash watching the market skyrocket without us, thinking surely it will correct soon and allow a window of opportunity, but it doesn't.

My advice here is to invest to beat inflation over the long term. But expect that it'll go down 20% tomorrow, so you're prepared. Expect the best but plan for the worst. That's my investing motto.

THE RIGHT AMOUNT OF RISK

This means we dial in a certain amount of risk while keeping enough money safe to weather the storm. This mix will be different for different people with different goals, at different stages, and with different tolerances for volatility. Generally, the younger you are, the more risk you can take. As we get closer to needing to withdraw funds for our goal, we should back off to a safer stance. But we're all different. Over time, you'll learn your tolerance for risk and know what kind of market volatility you can stand and still sleep at night.

How do we reduce risk in our portfolio? Very simply, we use our bond basket as a governor to reduce exposure to stocks down to an acceptable level. Using bonds in this way is not a perfect solution, but it's the simplest, most tried and true solution. Sometimes bonds and stocks move in tandem, and sometimes they don't. The important thing to remember about investment grade bonds (I don't ever use junk bonds) is that their volatility will be extremely low compared to the stock market. For example, the 60% stock and 40% bond portfolio I used as an example earlier in the chapter is a perfect starting point. Consider this a middle of the road normal investment mix that should over time outpace inflation effectively while still somewhat holding value during downturns.

Think of it this way. Let's say you have $1 million invested, and you're in retirement, pulling $36,000 per year out of the portfolio to live on. The market takes a massive dive, and that 60% or $600,000 of stock suddenly becomes $300,000. Ouch. As illustrated previously, the last thing you want to do is cash out of any of your stocks while they are down, even for living expenses. Over time, the stock portion of your portfolio will bounce back, but you need to let it. That's where the bonds come in. The 40% or $400,000 of bond hypothetically provides more than 10 years of money to live off of, if it takes that long for your stocks to recover. (But it won't, not even close.)

Based on your age, you can take more risk than that if you want. If you're 30 years old, you should invest your retirement portfolio as aggressively as you can handle. You'll see several market cycles before you ever make your first withdrawal, so you should go for it. If you are feeling confident and aggressive, shoot to have around 80 to 90% stock with a corresponding bond allocation. If you are prone to worry or anxiety, back off and stay more conservative. It's not worth losing sleep over, but try as best you can to maintain most of your retirement savings as equities if you're young.

Yet another important consideration when determining your stock–bond mix is your goal. How much money do you need to have at what age to retire successfully? Once you back into the savings needed to achieve what you want, you may want to adjust your portfolio to match the required return.

Let's say you're way ahead of the curve. Congrats! You could de-risk your portfolio by shifting some of your equities to bonds. Why not? Or, if you are behind, you should consider pushing yourself to take a little more risk during accumulation in order to increase the probability of reaching your goal.

EXPENSES

Previously we discussed the various ways my industry can very quickly create for you enough expenses that they deep-six your return. *Don't let that happen.* The first step is to stay away from any advisor who sells any commission products at all, period. If you can accomplish this, you are almost all the way there.

You are going to want to use either mutual funds or exchange-trad-ed funds (ETFs) to build your portfolio. If you have a fairly large portfolio, you may end up with individual stock and bond posi-tions, but for the average investor individual positions are not nec-essary or recommended. These mutual funds and ETFs all have an expense ratio that is clearly published and easy to find on the internet. Traditionally, the average expense ratio for no-load (no commission) funds has been around 0.7% to 1.4%. Therefore, if a fund makes 8% return and the expense ratio is 0.7%, then you made 7.3% after expenses. Get it? These days, expense ratios con-tinue to come way down. This is mainly because so many funds are operating more as either index funds or as baskets of unman-aged stocks that meet certain broad criteria.

If you work with a fee-only advisor, also previously mentioned, expect to have to pay him or her too. Generally, expect around 1%, depending upon the size of the portfolio and what level of service is being provided. For example, I currently charge 90 basis points on a $1.2-million portfolio, but that includes asset management *and* comprehensive financial planning. In addition, my clients currently incur an average of 0.25% of cost on the mutual funds we use, for a total cost of approximately 1.15% all in.

ACTIVE VS. PASSIVE

I'm sure you have seen the debate around active vs. passive investing in the media. It wasn't too long ago that Wall Street openly laughed and scoffed at those who embraced passive investing. Active investing is a fund where its managers pick the stocks to buy. Passive investing is just a fund that buys an entire index and makes no decisions. For years now, investor money has been steadily flowing from Wall Street's traditional, high-cost, actively managed funds to the newer, low-cost, passive alternatives. They are not laughing anymore. Some Wall Street firms purchased passive platforms and joined the ranks while others stood firm, insisting their stock-picking prowess is worth paying for.

Who is right? We can't be sure. There are plenty of studies that prove over and over how difficult it is for a mutual fund to outperform its index. Even more frustrating, these studies continue to demonstrate the impossibility of determining which funds will outperform the others going forward. Yet, there are a small handful of actively managed funds that have outperformed over long periods of time. Is their performance due to luck or skill? We'll probably never know for sure because statistically it would take more years than the career of any manager to make a good determination.

I think the most significant factor in the active vs. passive debate is cost, but this is correcting itself to a certain degree. Active funds are coming down in cost in order to compete. This is great for investors. Secondarily, since truly passive funds only try to replicate an index, I wonder if this is what we really want in our portfolios. Do I want to exactly replicate the S&P 500 in my portfolio? Not necessarily. The idea to me is more about trying to capture returns smartly with the least amount of risk. This means I should probably try to do better than just buying an S&P 500 index fund or ETF but with an eye towards keeping my costs in line.

Let's Go

Getting started is the hardest part. My advice here is to go for it and invest your money the best way you can with the resources available to you. That is how I first got started. Newly married and fresh out of college, I dabbled in individual stocks for a while until I realized it was a monster of a time suck. The complexity took over all of my free time and brain space. That's when I went on autopilot. After a little bit of research, I decided to automatically invest a small amount each month into the Gabelli Growth Fund, a no-load mutual fund that looked pretty good to me at the time.

If you are just getting started, you can do the same thing with any number of no-load mutual fund companies out there. Just pick one and go. You can switch later. Now there are more sophisticated, online automatic investing solutions, like Betterment, where you can create a fully diversified portfolio with a very low minimum initial investment. Don't make it complicated. Just start, and next thing you know, you'll be further along than you would have been otherwise.

At some point, you may want more personalized attention and care than just a login and monthly statement. This means you're going to go out and hire a real person to help out. Search out and find the best person for your family. Don't just settle for the young, nice kid who knocks on your door, the gal in the side office at your bank, or the firm that sponsors your favorite golf tournament.

That's going *backwards*. Next thing you know, you'll find yourself in mediocre investment instruments that benefit everybody up the chain but you. Do your research and seek out a fiduciary fee only advisor who will work for you.

RETIREMENT PLANS

For many people, their first foray into the world of investing is thrust upon them in the form of a retirement plan at work, most commonly a 401(k). There are a host of different retirement plans out there, called by many names, but if you are being asked by your employer to elect to have a certain percentage of your pay deducted and invested for your benefit, your plan is some kind of defined contribution plan with 401(k) provisions. Defined contribution simply means that the values, rules, and limits are defined by how much is contributed, either by you or by your employer.

There is also a lesser-used choice called a defined benefit plan. It is the opposite of a defined contribution plan, where the values are defined by how much benefit will be available to you in retirement. Defined benefit plans have declined in popularity over the last 30 years or so due to their complexity and cost to administer.

Defined contribution plans are more common today than they ever have been. What does this mean for you and me? It means that if we ever want to have enough money to stop working, then we have to actively decide to have money set aside and invest for that day. Nobody is going to do it for us.

Most employers dangle a carrot and offer to match some of the money you decide to invest as an incentive. Take the match, as much as they offer, but don't stop there. A common mistake many people make is that they let their employer define for them what they are going to contribute. For example, your employer may match dollar for dollar up to 3% of pay, meaning if you defer 3% of your check, they will add another 3% of your check, for a total of 6% of pay going into your retirement account. Is 6% the right number? Will 6% get you where you want to go? Probably not. As I mentioned previously, you need to know how much you need to be saving to meet your goal.

What I have found is that most people readily recognize the benefits of tax-advantaged savings in qualified retirement plans, IRAs, Roth IRAs, and even HSAs, but then they stop there. In other words, when they max out their employer's match or the deduction or contribution limits, they don't save any more. They just stop, and that's a mistake. If we stop there, we are letting our employer, or the tax laws define *for us* what our financial future will be.

In most cases, just maxing out employer match or deduction opportunities is not enough to achieve reasonable financial independence or retirement goals. Yet, in some other cases, I've seen people inadvertently overcontribute to their retirement plans and leave other important financial goals unmet. Don't let the results of your hard-earned savings be arbitrary. Rather, determine what you want to achieve and back into the savings that will be required. If you do this, you'll end up saving some money for long term purposes outside of retirement accounts.

Your retirement plan will have a set menu of investment choices for you to decide how to invest your money. Some employers have great investment options, others do not. Make the best of what is available and choose a path.

Many people who are not familiar with investing get caught here and end up not doing anything because they don't understand the different investment options. Don't get caught. Ask for help and information so you can make a good decision. If you are still unsure, hire a fee only advisor to review your options and provide a recommendation.

Deduct and Forget or Make It Automatic

It's not the tax treatment, the investment options, or even your employer's contributions that make your retirement plan such a great investment vehicle. Rather, it's the regular, automatic deductions that are the magic, the special sauce. Over time, no matter what is going on, or what expenses you are incurring in your household, these deductions are happening week in and week out.

You don't have to think about it; it just happens. Weeks go by, followed by months, years, and decades. Potentially one decision you make can create hundreds of transactions over your working lifetime in order for you to accumulate more than would ever be possible any other way. Unless it gets screwed up somehow.

The Evil Bad Guy Called "Life"

While these regular contributions are being made, we are living our crazy lives. Medical emergencies, divorce, college expenses, employment termination, you name it; we have to deal with all of this stuff. It's like having a bad guy who periodically arrives and steals some of your money. Try to maintain adequate cash reserves to deal with challenges and, most importantly, protect your retirement accounts from any and all immediate needs. I'm sure there is a good reason out there somewhere to take money out of a retirement plan early, but I haven't seen it.

When you change jobs, the temptation to distribute the balance to yourself can be overwhelming. Transitions, like job transitions, are when we need money more than any other time. But your retirement accounts are for retirement, and your cash reserves are for emergencies, opportunities, and transitions. Once we start using money saved for one purpose to fulfill another, everything gets screwed up. Instead of distributing your retirement account to yourself in the form of a check when changing jobs, you should either roll your funds into your new retirement plan or into an

IRA. Either way, this preserves the preferential tax treatment of your funds and allows you to continue to invest for retirement.

Just like most people's first investment is in their company's 401(k) or retirement plan, usually their second investment account is an IRA or Roth IRA. Over time, your IRA and Roth IRA will collect retirement funds from your retirement accounts. Depending on your income, marital status, and retirement plan eligibility, you may be able to make contributions directly to your IRA, Roth IRA, or both.

Once you have established an IRA and Roth, there are a number of strategies you can use to fill these buckets, such as converting assets from your IRA to your Roth, based upon several factors and conditions. These strategies are beyond the scope of this book and can change from year to year with the tax laws. The main point here is that you should establish IRAs and Roth IRAs as part of your family's long-term retirement investment strategy.

OPEN YOUR GENERAL INVESTMENT ACCOUNT NOW

But what about money for other goals, besides retirement? You'll need to open a general investment account. You can start an account by investing directly with a mutual fund company like I did when I first started investing in the Gabelli Growth Fund in 1989. Or, you can use some of the investment advice I suggested, open an account at Betterment, and be fully diversified across the wide spectrum of asset classes. Finally, if you want a customized, more personalized experience, you can hire a fee only advisor, like me.

However you start, your general investment account will, over time, become a very important piece of your financial picture. Because there are no real tax advantages, like with IRAs, etc., you don't have to comply with all of the rules like tax penalties for early withdrawals, required minimum distributions, or any of that silly stuff. This means your general investment account is very flexible compared to the rest of your money.

Because of the flexibility, you'll want to invest this account differently. Most people will invest more conservatively in their general investment account. If you need money sooner rather than later, you want less volatile investments that can be liquidated more easily for medium-term goals like college for kids, housing, weddings, etc. Note that this is not your emergency cash money. Rather, this account is invested for longer-term wealth accumulation.

SUMMARY

Looking back at the performance of the stock market over time, it looks easy. All we have to do is invest a good portion of our funds in stocks, and we should be able to beat inflation soundly to attain our goals. But it's not easy. Retirement investing is the hardest easy investing there is. Our future depends upon our success, so there is a chance we could freak out and let our very human fear derail us at any point. Just like my duck hunting trips where my own missteps became my worst enemies.

There is a lot of noise to deal with too. All of the fancy jargon and market talk we are constantly bombarded with does nothing to help us achieve long-term success. It's easy to forget what stock is, what it represents, and how we as long-term investors should properly deploy stock in the face of all of the noise, confusion, and volatility. The key is to not be discouraged, to continue to steadily invest, and to remember it's a distance race against inflation. Investing this way has allowed me some leisure time, so I can go out early in the morning with my son and sit in cold, wet ponds with soaked feet. Sound like fun?

Chapter 8

WHEN ENOUGH IS ENOUGH

"I think we're going to be able to call it," Austin says as we review our clients financial plan and assets on the big screen in my office. We've been running and rerunning the scenarios, carefully reviewing possible future expenses and expected returns. We adjust for different inflation scenarios, stress test against market crashes, model untimely deaths, and add in rising healthcare costs.

Our software hums along, churning out thousands of simulations based upon past market conditions and fluctuations. "There's an 83% probability of success," I say as the Monte Carlo simulation completes its analysis. "Not bad, I think we have it." We're excited. Tomorrow, when our clients come in, we'll call it.

For us, calling it is the culmination and ultimate result of years of work with a client. The day we call it is the day our client could, if they wanted to, quit their paying gig and live comfortably on their accumulated assets. Calling it spells freedom. True financial independence is the ultimate payoff from years of planning and implementation.

The funny thing is, most of the time when we call it for a client, they continue to work and achieve, sometimes for many years after their personal financial success has been cemented. But they work differently, with a different attitude, perspective, and a clearer sense of calling that may not have been there before. For many, the culmination of their life's work and accomplishments will occur *after* this moment. I think it's the freedom that personal financial success provides that becomes the impetus.

It's a privilege to be an active participant in such an amazing, life-changing process and event. But it's certainly different than it used to be. Retirement has changed over the years. The retirement of our parents, our grandparents or even our great-grandparents is probably completely different than what we will experience. Back in the day, as the Industrial Revolution took shape, people's bodies would just wear out over time in the factories and mills, and therefore they weren't worth much anymore in the workforce. Social Security and defined benefit pension plans were created to ease workers out to pasture in a humane fashion, so younger, healthier, and cheaper laborers could fill their slots.

The system worked, mainly because most people didn't live very long after retirement. I remember my grandad talking about his dad, my great-grandfather, who died in his easy chair two weeks after retiring from the factory in Houston where had worked his entire adult life. It also worked because our workforce was not very portable, meaning people worked for the same employer for many years, so an old-fashioned pension based upon years of service held value.

Fast forward to today, and we have very different dynamics in play. People live longer and need more money for a longer retirement. We also change jobs a lot more often than our parents or grandparents did, so defined contribution plans, such as 401(k)s, are more popular due to their portability. But most importantly, people often don't want to retire. And because of their knowledge and experience, many are still very much valued in the workplace.

These changing and shifting dynamics make retirement much more difficult to define and plan for. But they also make planning much, much more important. One of the greatest risks we face in retirement is running out of money before we die, so the longer we're expected to live, the more important it becomes to get our retirement assets squared away. The portable defined contribution retirement plans, or 401(k)s, most of us have now are our responsibility, not our employer's. In most cases, if there is going to be money available for us at retirement, it's up to us to individually make it happen.

Where is Social Security in all of this? It's there, and it's a relevant amount of money. But to get the best bang for your buck, you want to wait all the way to age 70 before you start drawing. But even then, for most of us, it's not enough money to live on comfortably. Many of my clients want to work as long as they can. They love their jobs. They are valued for their skills and are usually making more money than they ever have previously. They don't want to stop, but planning to work until you can't anymore is not a good way to go about it. You never know when that might be.

That's why I encourage anybody and everybody to work toward financial independence. Don't call it retirement if you don't want to, but financial independence is kind of the same thing. When we work toward financial independence, we are simply trying to accumulate enough money to where, if we didn't want to work or couldn't work, we would still be able to live the lifestyle we desire for ourselves.

I always loved the ING commercial where people are walking around with numbers over their heads. "What's your number?" the commercial would ask. It's true. Everybody has a number, and for everybody it's different. Your number depends on what your future expenses look like, your tolerance for risk with your investments, your health, and how adequate your health insurance and long-term care insurance may be. I've spent most of my adult life calculating this number for people and helping them achieve it.

Trying to sum up everything I know on this topic in one chapter is impossible. But hopefully I can provide some insight and guidance to help you along your path.

THE EARLIER THE BETTER

Hopefully, you can achieve financial independence at a young enough age, so you aren't just going off to pasture to die, like the old days. Rather, this independence should be an opportunity to maybe go do some things that you weren't able to do while you were working. Financial independence is something we should be excited about.

Many times, financial independence can be achieved in phases. Maybe you transition from 40 hours a week to 20 or work more as a consultant and less as an employee. Or maybe you sell a business to devote all of your time to your favorite charity. If you are healthy and enjoy what you do, why not keep doing it? Retirement does not have to be the end of your contributions to the economy or society. Far from it. Many of the people I know who are "retiring" these days see it more as the culmination of their life's experiences, where they feel more valued for who they are and what they do than ever before.

THE RIGHT ATTITUDE

Retirement should be fun. It should be something we're looking forward to and not something we're forced into due to circumstances beyond our control. That means we have to be purposeful about it and control what we can; that's retirement planning. If you enjoy your career, then find a way to continue doing what you love. If there are hobbies you enjoy, financial independence will allow you to enjoy them even more. Most of my retired clients travel like crazy. They have been so many places and had so much fun. Retirement allows you to travel during the off season to avoid the crowds.

Looooong

Many times, we joke in the office about what the perfect, most efficient retirement scenario looks like. On a graph, it's downward sloping, where your assets go from something to zero on the day that you die. Home run.

Of course, it's impossible to execute because we generally don't know what day we're going to die ahead of time. Mortality experts predict that many of those in the younger generations today could live to age 120 or beyond. That's crazy to think about, but scary too if you're a financial planner. This makes any kind of spend-down strategy a nonstarter. What I mean is, if people are going to live that long, once they achieve financial independence, they can't afford to spend their basis, or principal, at all.

Expensive

There are a lot of expenses that go away in retirement. Many of my clients pay off their house, so there's no mortgage to deal with. Taxes can go way down, since you're probably not pulling a paycheck anymore. Your kids are hopefully grown, out of the house, and financially independent from you.

But wait, what are you going to do with all of that free time you have? You're probably going to want to travel, entertain, and spend money on all sorts of fun things that you didn't have time for previously. This all usually happens in the first stage of retirement, which I call the honeymoon. It's fun, blissful, and invigorating. It's a carefree existence that makes you feel as if you are newly married, without a care in the world. It looks like fun to me, but you have to make sure you plan for these expenses.

Once the honeymoon is over, a second retirement stage emerges. I call it mature actualization. In this stage, the honeymoon is over, and you come back down out of the clouds. At this point, you become very aware of your mortality, your legacy, and what's truly important. Bonds with your closest friends and family become stronger than they have ever been before. You travel less and usually spend less money. If you have been blessed with significant, excess assets, many times this is when retirees become very comfortable with gifting to their family and favorite charitable causes.

HEALTH

The third and final phase of retirement is usually not nearly as fun and can be by far the most expensive phase of your entire life. No matter how careful we are with our bodies, eventually they wear out. In the third phase of retirement, we start to lose capabilities either physically, mentally, or both. This phase can be costly and stressful.

I've been through this phase with clients and, of course, parents and grandparents. It's tough on everybody. The key here is to make sure we planned on the expenses somehow, either through long-term care insurance or sufficient funds that have been set aside. Our lifeboat drills start to become the real thing. So it's good that we have talked through stuff, and everybody knows what they are supposed to do.

FINDING YOUR NUMBER AND UNDERSTANDING WHAT IT MEANS

Now you should have a clearer understanding of what retirement may or may not look like and a general picture of what your expenses might be during the different phases of retirement. Your retirement and associated expenses will be unique to you. There are no general rules of thumb that hold up very well in this regard. Initially, you can shoot for 80% replacement of current income, but that's a shot in the dark. What income? Current income? How old are you, and what does that represent in future income dollars? Is your house paid off in retirement? What about health insurance? If you try to retire before age 65, then you are not Medicare eligible yet. What are you going to do about health insurance, and how much is it going to cost?

See what I mean? Modern financial planning software is designed to take all of these considerations into account, and modern financial planners know how to read and interpret what the software is saying, in order to make sound recommendations. But to give you a general idea, let's do some easy math and make some broad assumptions.

THE RULE OF 72 AND THE 4% RULE

The rule of 72 is a great way to calculate the growth of investments over time and the erosion of purchasing power by inflation. Unfortunately, it does not provide any insight into cash flow streams, like steady periodic investing or distributions, but the 4% rule helps out on safe distribution amounts. Let's say you crunched some numbers and, in today's dollars, you think you could live off of $9,000 per month in retirement. Social Security is projected to provide $3,000 per month in income in today's dollars. That means you need to figure out how to generate $6,000 per month, or $72,000 for the first year of retirement. Since Social Security is indexed to inflation, you can assume that you will only have to account for inflation on your additional income need. This means that for the next year, you'll need, let's say, 3% more to keep up with inflation.

The mistake a lot of people make here is that they take an assumed return and call it income. For example, let's say you have decided you will invest 60% of your money in stocks and 40% in income. Taking into account historical data, you think you can make, on average, 6% per year. If you divide $72,000 by 6%, you get $1.2 million. This means that $1.2 million could potentially provide $72,000 per year of income for the rest of your life as long as you don't touch the principal. But let's say you are estimating that you'll live 24 years in retirement. This calculation does not properly take into account inflation.

So, assume 3% inflation. The rule of 72 says that if we divide 72 by a factor, it will give the number of years it will take for that

117

factor to double with compounding. This is super handy. 3 goes into 72 a total of 24 times. This means that in 24 years, you'll need $144,000 per year in income to match the purchasing power of $72,000 in income today, all due to inflation.

Financial planning software takes all of this into account and then some, but there is another handy rule of thumb called the 4% rule that we can use for quick and dirty estimates of what your initial retirement balance needs to be in order to keep up with inflation. Planning geeks like me argue the validity of the 4% rule with each other constantly, and most of us have shifted to more dynamic withdrawal guidelines. But more on that later. The 4% rule says that if you divide a moderately invested portfolio (like the one in this example) by 4%, you should be able to withdraw that amount safely and increase it each year to keep up with inflation during retirement. And $72,000 divided by 4% gives us $1.8 million as our target number, not $1.2 million.

So, is that your number? Nope. Remember, that's your number if you retired today. Let's say you are still 24 years out. If that's the case, we have to adjust your number for inflation. Using our rule of 72 calculation, that's one doubling period for inflation again. If we double the present value calculation, we get $2.4 million. Now *that's* finally your number.

Now that we know the future account balance value needed to retire comfortably, we can use a financial calculator to calculate what it's going to take to get there. Assuming a 6% return, if your current 401(k) balance is $250,000, you'll need to contribute a little over $2,100 per month for the next 24 years to achieve your goal. This is an illustration only, and the numbers will change drastically based upon your circumstances.

I hope all of that makes sense. There are lots of steps to calculating retirement income needs and so many factors to consider. There are a number of good retirement calculation tools on the internet that can get you pointed in the right direction, but at some point, it will probably make sense to have a financial planner run all of it for you.

RETIREMENT INCOME IS A LONG-TERM GOAL THESE DAYS

You may have noticed that I used a moderate mix of stocks and bonds, both for the portfolio assumption during accumulation *and* during retirement. However, you may have read elsewhere that we are supposed to reduce our reliance on stocks and shift to a safer portfolio as we get older and retire. I don't subscribe to that theory, and here's why. First of all, with longer life expectancies, retirement income becomes just as much of a fight against inflation as it is while saving for retirement. Granted, inflation has been low in recent years, but so have interest rates. If we convert our portfolio to mostly or entirely bonds, we won't generate nearly enough money to maintain a good income stream.

Our best weapon against inflation is a diversified portfolio that includes a good amount of stocks or stock funds. So, keeping stocks in our retirement portfolio after retiring will increase the probability of our money lasting to the end. But more stocks in our portfolio also increases volatility.

This means that, some years, our retirement portfolio will do phenomenally well and in other years it will lose money. How do we deal with this? I think one way we deal with it is by adjusting some of the assumptions we made when coming up with our withdrawal rate. Instead of just calculating 4% of $2.4 million in our example and blindly increasing that income amount by inflation every year, we have to insert some common sense. We can choose to forgo the annual inflation increase, and only increase your income withdrawal every few years, when you feel things are getting tight. We can also recalculate our withdrawal rate against the ending balance annually.

So, for example, if after the first year of retirement you end up with fantastic returns and the balance increases by $100,000, even after your withdrawals, then take 4% of that number and give yourself a raise. If, in the next year, your portfolio loses money and the balance goes down, adjust your income down accordingly. Heck, isn't this what we do our whole lives? When times are good, we go to Disneyland; when they're not, we pack it up and drive to Galveston for summer vacation instead. Why should retirement be any different? Don't think of your retirement income as fixed income, that concept does not hold up under modern market conditions.

In Closing

In closing out this important chapter, I want to get away from the math of retirement and back into the attitude and mindset we should all be striving for if we want to retire successfully. Here are my five most important tips:

1. If you are miserable now, retirement will probably not make you happy. Retirement is not the solution if you don't enjoy your job. Too often we set ourselves up for unrealistic expectations when we are not happy with our current lives. Focus on doing the things you enjoy in your job to get your attitude in shape. Looking to retirement as a solution to all of your problems is dangerous and unrealistic.

2. Practice your retirement today while you are still working. Take time off and do the things you see yourself doing in retirement. Whether it is volunteering, travelling, or consulting you should not wait to try these things on for size. Like with anything, if you practice it makes you better. Heck, you might discover you *hate* travelling. Better to know now.

3. Talk it out with your spouse and your planner. By far the best meetings that happen in my office are the ones where the husband, wife, and I walk through the retirement process. Everybody needs to be onboard, communicating, and engaged early on in order for everything to work out successfully.

4. Plan on being busy, maybe busier than you are today. Know your priorities and values, so you can make good decisions with your time. Just like any other stage of your life, your time will be a valuable commodity, so use it wisely toward the things that really matter.

5. Make your health a top priority. I am seeing more and more studies that demonstrate good health as the top predictor of a successful retirement. Unfortunately, our bodies eventually wear out and things (long-term care, hospitalization, medications) get expensive. Take care of your body so you can maximize the fun part of retirement and minimize healthcare costs.

Chapter 9

KIDS AND MONEY, BUT NOT JUST COLLEGE MONEY

Shelly and I have four kids. Somehow, all four have grown up to become wonderful, smart, and successful young adults. I'm sure we had something to do with it, but it was when we allowed our kids to find their own way that we did some of our best parenting.

I'm not a very emotional person, but there have been what I consider to be monumental moments in each of my kids' lives that have made me bawl like a baby. Gretchen, our oldest, is extremely smart. I was proud when she was accepted into one of the most prestigious architecture programs in the country. But it didn't work out, and she was soon back home from New York City. Broken, depressed, and without any clear direction, she scraped herself up off the ground and slowly worked her way back on track. Later, when she walked across the stage at College Park Center at The University of Arlington to accept her degree, to me it represented not as much what she had achieved but, rather, more what she overcame. I could not have been more proud of her than I was at that moment, and she has gone on to achieve advanced degrees and great success in a career she loves.

Grace, our number two, is a real go-getter. As a youngster, she loved volleyball more than anything and worked hard at it. She would go on to achieve record-setting performance in college, but high school ball was a struggle. Her coach was especially tough on her, too tough. Grace endured overwhelming pressure and negativity. She struggled and fought hard to overcome. At the end of her senior year, it all came together as she dominated the middle of the court and tasted sweet, hard-fought success. Just like with Gretchen, to me her success was so much more than what you saw on the court. It represented her own personal fight against the odds.

Just like any parent, I hate to see my kids struggle, yet looking back, I know that they grew when they failed a little. Our two youngest kids, Daniel and Gwen, have both had to deal with career-ending sports injuries. But those two are amazing. They both bounced back from their setbacks, found new passions, new dreams, and learned to overcome.

Of course, as parents we need to do everything we can to create a safe environment for our children. But we can go way overboard. I'm sure you are familiar with the term "helicopter parent." You know, hovering over and trying to protect our kids from everything. Now, with the big college admissions scandal that hit in 2019, some big names in the entertainment industry got to do some time in the big house for taking it to the next level. They have defined the latest crop of "lawnmower parents" who mow down every obstacle in their child's path, no matter the cost.

But the ultimate cost is potentially never allowing our kids to grow up at all and destroying our own finances in the process. Over the years, I have worked with couples who, nearing their own retirement, are still financially supporting their adult kids. That's ridiculous. Sure, there are circumstances and events that may require us to step in and financially help out a struggling adult child, but ongoing financial support for healthy adult children is not in anybody's best interests, theirs or ours. It's from this perspective, then, that trying to teach our kids how to be adults instead of protecting them from being adults makes the most sense in our quest to help them financially succeed.

Too often, we worry about the wrong things and miss the point. Many of my clients state a strong desire to pass on money to their kids. That's great, but I always ask, "Why?" Sometimes they answer; "Because we want them not to worry or struggle the way we did, and we want them to be happy." Others answer with, "Because that's what our parents did for us, and we want our money to be a lasting family legacy."

Ask yourself, "Why?" Your answer will reveal some important insight into how to move forward with regard to money and your kids. More often than not, it can help us realize these two important factors:

1. Never talking about money with your kids, not being honest about money with them, and treating it as a taboo subject the way that most families do is a really bad idea.

2. Spending all of your time planning and setting up a brilliantly tax-efficient trust strategy that transfers all of your wealth at your death with a multitude of strings and spendthrift provisions probably misses the point.

One of the best gifts we can give to our children from a financial standpoint is to ensure that they don't have to take care of us financially in our old age. This means getting our own financial house in order should be our priority. From there, I think our next step should be to focus on financial education.

Adult Training

One of the hardest parts of being an adult is learning all of the ins and outs of financial responsibility. I know for most of us, we had to figure it all out on our own, but it doesn't have to be that way.

We should educate our kids early about how to value and properly handle money, and the best way to do it is through a good old-fashioned allowance. Executed properly, an allowance teaches kids all of the basics.

An allowance is a critical step toward their eventual financial independence, so it's important to keep this future goal in mind when devising an allowance strategy. The general concept is to ensure our kids already have some money handling skills before they leave for college and beyond. Once they are out of the house, you lose power and insight into what they are doing with their money, and you lose the ability to help. Here are some of my do's and don'ts when it comes to allowances:

Do...

- Have your child create the budget. Before handing over funds, ask your kid to make up a list of what they need money for and how much. I will almost guarantee they will grossly undershoot their actual need because they do not have a clue what things cost. Work with them to come up with realistic numbers and use their budget as a guide for their initial allowance amount. Periodically, get together with your child and make adjustments as necessary.

- Hold the line. If the agreement is for them to buy their own clothes, resist bailing them out if they initially blow all of their money on movies and dinners with friends. Provide your child with the opportunity to feel the consequences of their spending decisions. It's better for them to learn about these consequences now instead of later, when you're not around to provide guidance and support.

- Have your child set up a checking and savings account. Instead of just handing over cash, go ahead and help your kid learn about banking. I would suggest both a checking and savings account. Teach them to use the checking account for regular monthly expenditures, like gas, and to use their savings account for periodic purchases, like clothes and car repairs.

Don't...

- Use an allowance as a control or discipline device. A well-devised allowance plan is just the opposite of control. The allowance should allow your child the freedom to make some of their own choices and exert some independence. Remember, we're training our kids to be responsible adults not enforcing our will upon them.

- Play "good parent, bad parent." Make sure the guidelines of what your child is responsible for, like clothes and gas, are clearly established and adhered to by both parents. Healthy spending habits will not burgeon if the only thing your child needs to do when they want extra cash is go see Dad.

- Tie an allowance to chores or duties. This is a controversial one, but I'm going with it anyway. Everybody in the household should have duties they are expected to complete. Money has little to do with the roles that family members play to support one another. Think of an allowance as an extension of the financial support we already provide to our children, only we are providing it in a way that teaches them a skill.

It's astounding to me how easily kids pick up great money habits when we approach their training with the right attitude and keep these guidelines in mind. If your kid can establish sound money handling habits early on, it will drastically improve their prospects for a financially sound future. In my opinion, this kind of training is more important and more effective than gifting strategies or inheritance. As the old proverb says, "Give a man a fish, and you feed him for a day. Teach a man to fish, and you feed him for a lifetime."

But each kid responds differently to allowance training. One of my kids is a natural-born saver and investor. Because she has been handling her own money for some time now, she was able to discover this trait and become diligent and successful with her money at a very young age. Another one of my kids loves, loves, loves to spend. Fortunately, she learned this about herself early on and has done an incredible job putting saving and investing on autopilot, so she never has the chance to spend it.

SET REALISTIC EXPECTATIONS

I often see parents make mistakes when it comes to their children and the great college search. You need to be honest with them about your financial constraints. We all want what's best for our kids, so ideally, we want them to be able to go where they want for higher education. But tuition has skyrocketed over the years. Thirty years ago, sending a kid off to a college campus to "find herself" in the "college experience" did not cost what it does today. To justify today's inflated tuition bills, there needs to be an endgame career plan that's worth the cost. So, we need to ask our children why they want to go to college and why they want to go to that specific school. They need to verbalize a desire with sound reasoning in order to justify the costs.

More and more, my clients and their kids are discovering ways to achieve a great career path without college being a part of the equation at all. The job market is much more specialized than it used to be. Skills like graphic design, acting, or even robotic technology do not necessarily require college degrees. Good communication about what your child wants to do, along with sound research and planning, can open up new, fun, and creative ways for your child to achieve their dreams.

Case in point, Michael Dell was one year ahead of me at the University of Texas. College was not his thing, so he dropped out to assemble and sell computers. By the time I graduated, Dell Inc. was a publicly listed company on the NASDAQ. He had a great idea. But more importantly, his timing was perfect. The opportunity costs Michael would have paid for finishing his college career just because "that's what you're supposed to do" are staggering. It takes courage to forge your own path and not just go with the flow, but it can really pay off.

STUDENT LOANS

Of course, it's best to avoid student loans. I had a young couple come see me recently. They both had great incomes and careers but were struggling financially. Once we dug into their financials, we found their student debt was strangling them. It kept them from being able to afford decent housing, save sufficiently for retirement, or save for *their* kid's college. What a shame. There is around $1.5 trillion dollars of outstanding student debt out there[4] causing financial troubles for another 50 million American adults, just like the young couple who met with me. The financial ripple effect of all of this is beyond my comprehension and could severely impact these families for generations.

Even with the skyrocketing costs, if you are creative and work at it, I think college can still happen for our kids without breaking the bank or putting them hopelessly in debt. For one, there are so many college options. Instead of just blindly defaulting to your alma mater, do some research and see if you can find the schools that are looking for a kid like yours. These days, college shopping is kind of like car shopping. Many times, there is the sticker price, but then there are discounted tuition amounts for kids who meet

---

4 Ben Miller, Colleen Campbell, Brent J. Cohen, and Charlotte Hancock, "Addressing the $1.5 Trillion in Federal Student Loan Debt," Center for American Progress, June 12, 2019, https://www.americanprogress.org/issues/education-postsecondary/reports/2019/06/12/470893/addressing-1-5-trillion-federal-student-loan-debt/

certain SAT or GPA requirements. Aggressively pursue all scholarship opportunities.

To really save money, you can look into getting the basics out of the way at a local junior college. Our local junior college costs less than $1,800 per year. Better yet, encourage your child to take advanced placement or dual credit courses while in high school. I have a client whose daughter, Bethany, graduated from high school with 30 advanced placement credits. From there, she enrolled locally in the University of Texas at Arlington. Because of her grades and GPA, they waived 90% of her tuition. She hit it hard and graduated in two years, thanks to all of those advanced placement credits. She enrolled in law school well before her 21st birthday. Her parents were able to preserve all of her college savings since her undergraduate degree was almost free (not to mention only two years instead of four), so it could be used for law school. That's being smart about it.

College is not the only big-ticket item on the menu when it comes to raising kids. Don't forget about cars and weddings, or even some assistance with their first home. If you want to help provide any of these items, you'll need to plan ahead.

PLANNING TO PAY FOR COLLEGE (OR CARS, OR WEDDINGS, OR…)

For most of us, if there is going to be money available to pay for all of this, we'll have to formulate a plan. Modern financial planning software does a great job of integrating these expenses into an overall long-term financial plan. With software, we are able to take into account a family's income, expenses, and overall savings capabilities in order to provide recommendations.

In running these plans over the years, here are some general ideas and concepts I have found to be helpful. First off, as we already discussed, college is expensive, and tuition rates continue to increase much faster than normal inflation. I usually assume a 6%

increase in tuition costs. That's so high that you can skip the time value of money calculations completely and just assume that college expenses will go up at the same rate as your assumed return.

For this reason, the first time you run a calculation to solve for how much you need to sock away monthly for your kids' college to meet 100% of the cost, prepare to be shocked and depressed. In most cases, it's unattainable. But after you pull yourself off of the floor, open a college savings account and start saving what you can anyway. If you can't fund the whole enchilada right now, that's okay. Any amount you save will be needed and will provide important options.

The amazing thing to me about college planning is that in spite of all of the challenges, it nearly always works out. I don't mean you just finance college with student loans and worry about it later. No, it works out if you're smart about it, communicate effectively, and set realistic expectations. I can't say this about retirement planning. In planning for retirement, if we're not marching along in step with a plan, disaster usually strikes. I think it's because, although college is expensive, it's not nearly as expensive as retirement.

An average couple with a child going off to college this year should expect four years to cost somewhere between $60,000 and $100,000.[5] That's pretty rough, but retirement might be a short 15 years away with a $2.4 million price sticker on it. Don't let college planning take you off track for your retirement planning.

How do most of my clients make college work out effectively? They pay for a lot of it out of current income. There are some expenses in the home (activities, eating out) that diminish when Junior goes away to college, and those expenses get redirected to his tuition. In addition, it seems that right around college time,

---

5 Katie Lobosco, "No Scholarship? Here's How to Pay for College," *CNN* online, May 5, 2017, https://money.cnn.com/2017/04/25/pf/college/pay-for-college/index.html

mom and dad start hitting full stride in their careers. Age, experience, and less time hauling kids all over tarnation translates into higher wages at this juncture, part of which gets thrown into the college cauldron.

WHERE TO PUT IT

If you Google "college savings plans," the number 529 comes up. A 529 plan is a tax-advantaged college savings account, kind of similar to an IRA. If you save for college inside of a 529 plan, the earnings are tax free as long as they are used for college-related expenses. These accounts have a lot of flexibility, but if the money is not used for college, you usually have to pay ordinary income taxes on the gains along with a 10% penalty, though there are some exceptions.

I don't get overly excited about 529 plans. First off, the timeframe between saving for college and paying for college is relatively short compared to other long-term investing, like retirement. This means there is not as much time for tax-advantaged savings to make a significant difference in the ending balance. In other words, the juice is not worth the squeeze.

My preference is to save for college in a plain old, simple investment account, in your name so that you can do whatever you want. That way, the money can be used for a multitude of expenses, not just college. The great news here is, if you are able to get your kids through school and preserve some of your "college" savings, it can be used for a wedding, as a down payment for their first home, or my favorite, you can keep if for yourself as part of your retirement plan.

That being said, there are a couple of instances where I like 529 plans. When my client has a lump sum of money and we want to preserve and protect it specifically for college, a 529 plan is the way to go. Contributions into a 529 plan are considered a gift. This means the funds will be protected from creditors or lawsuits against you. Usually, you can only gift a certain amount per year, currently $15,000 per donor per donee, without having to pay gift and estate tax. But with a 529 plan, you can give more. It's called superfunding, and you can contribute up to five years' worth of gifts in a single year. This means a couple can make a single $150,000 contribution into a 529 plan for a child without paying gift tax. A large single lump sum like that early on makes the tax-free return of a 529 plan look pretty enticing all of the sudden. I call this the one-and-done approach to college planning.

But here's an even better way to superfund college: get the grand-parents involved. Grandparents often want to help out with college, but they are unsure or wary of doing so. If the grandparents fund a 529, it's kind of like a free trust. It's a gift directly to the grandchild for a specific purpose. It has to be used for college, is protected from creditors or divorce, and can even be transferred to another grandkid if circumstances dictate.

If you are self-employed, you may have the opportunity to fund college on a tax-deductible basis by hiring your kids in your business. If they are under age 18, you don't have to pay payroll taxes on their paychecks, so hire them to do some work for you in your business, then turn around and use that money later for college. Even if they are over 18 and you have to pay payroll taxes, I think it can still be worth it. I hired one of my daughters while she was in college to manage social media postings for me. She used those funds for her living expenses, and they were tax deductible for me.

INHERITANCE

Eventually if there is anything left, your kids will probably end up with your money. But unfortunately, the odds of your kids being successful with that money are extremely low. Some studies show that, 70% of the time, family money vaporizes by the next generation.[6] I believe it. Early in my career, I had the opportunity

---

6 Amy A. Castoro, "Wealth Transition and Entitlement: Shedding Light on the Dark Side

to work hand in hand with a well-heeled trust department in one of our local banks. Most of the trust clients were multi-generation wealth heirs, and for the most part, they didn't have a clue about anything. "What a terrible way to exist," I thought at the time. Most of these clients were completely set up financially. They didn't have to do much, so they didn't. I decided right then and there that I wouldn't do something like that to my children.

Due to my experience with these trust department clients, I now work hard to help my clients raise their kids to be financially responsible, capable of handling money in a way that is fulfilling for them and beneficial to society. We aggressively pursue a strategy of financial education with our client's children. We have what we call kid meetings, where their children come in and we discuss the financial aspects of being an adult. This generally happens first right around the time they start driving, and we talk about budgeting, allowances, and college expectations. From there, we try to be an open door for them as they go off to college and take on more financial responsibility for themselves. Then, when they get their first job, we try to be there to help them with their savings and retirement plan decisions. Finally, we try to make it easy for them to engage with us as clients, with no minimum asset requirements and waived planning fees. Why do we do this? Because eventually they will have their parent's money, and if we can help them learn a thing or two about financial responsibility now, hopefully they won't screw it up.

This approach flies in the face of the approach my trust officer compadres take. In contrast, they build out these complicated and expensive trusts and such with all kinds of restrictions, safeguards, trip wires, and provisions. I think that's kind of like when your kid is about to turn 16, and they get their first car. That's scary, so what do many parents do? They do research and buy the safest

of a Charmed Life," The Journal of Wealth Management 18, no. 2 (Fall 2015): http://www. phase3.biz/core/userfiles/TWG/files/JWM_Fall_2015_WG.pdf car on the market, fully equipped with 20 airbags, state of the art crumple zones, lane departure, dashcams, and crash notification systems. But what good is all of that if you never properly trained your child to drive safely in the first place? The key to staying safe on the road is not safety technology, it's good, safe driving skills. The key to making inherited funds last is teaching our kids sound financial skills.

Teaching financial responsibility skills to our kids is critically important to their long-term success, yet few parents really even try. It's sad. You can have a brilliant kid who goes off to MIT and becomes a successful doctor. But if he or she never learned any money skills, there is a decent chance they will never achieve personal financial success. Heck, add a big portfolio of student loans to the mix, and they are practically doomed. I see it all of the time.

Chapter 10

LIFE'S FINAL CHAPTER

It was calm and quiet, early on a Tuesday morning. I had just arrived at my desk in old Steindam Hall on the University of Texas campus. Newly married, graduated, and freshly commissioned in the US Navy, I was stashed there, as the Navy calls it, in my old ROTC unit, waiting on orders that would soon take Shelly and I far away to Newport, Rhode Island for my first duty assignment.

The big, old analog phone on my desk jumped to life, piercing the morning's serenity like an alarm clock. I paused and waited for the second ring as was customary back then. A dull thunk followed, as I pushed in the blinking button at the bottom of my phone labelled "Line 1" and answered in my best grown-up military voice, "Ensign Schulz." "Hey, it's Nick," came the reply from the other end. Then, in a low, somber tone, "I'm at your parents' house. You need to get over here, now."

That got my attention. Nicky Morris and I had been best friends since we were 10. At times, he had practically lived at my house. In recent years, he and his wife purchased a home just down the street. While I had been away at college, an early morning ritual between Nick and my dad had developed. On the way to work, Nick would turn the corner at Cecelia and Howard, drive past our old driveway, look over his shoulder, and wave at my dad, who was always there sitting on the back porch, waiting for the exchange.

But on this particular morning, as Nick turned his head there was something wrong. My dad was lying on the ground. He was gone. His heart had stopped suddenly. My mom was still asleep, so Nick was the first to realize what had happened.

"What's wrong?" I said, rather forcefully. "You just need to get here. It's your dad; you just need to get here, now." Poor Nick just couldn't say it. He probably still didn't even believe it. He didn't say it. I didn't make him say it. I just did what he said.

Everybody reacts to tragedy differently. I go numb. Everything slows down as my dulled senses throw up a wall to protect and isolate me from what's really happening. After 30 years, I still remember that phone call like it was yesterday, but the days that followed are a muffled blur. The Navy graciously provided me with two weeks of leave I hadn't yet earned. I tried to use that time as efficiently as I could to handle what needed to be done. It was not enough time, but I did what I could.

The timing of my dad's death was not good. My retired, 79-year-old grandfather still owned a majority stake in the family business where he worked. They were just coming out of an economic downturn. No transition plan existed, and my dad didn't have life insurance either personally or through the family newspaper. He did not have a pension plan or much in the way of invested assets at the time of his death. Nearly all of my parents' net worth was tied to their minority stake in the company. In other words, no plan existed for the unlikely and unforeseen circumstances that transpired. After going through every inch of my dad's mounds of papers and projects, we could not find his Last Will and Testament. Needless to say, settling my dad's estate proved to be a prolonged, agonizing, and expensive process with an end result that was to no one's satisfaction.

The morbid point of me telling such a painful and personal story is this: we all need to plan on dying. There's a 100% probability that it's going to happen at some point. When we plan for our kids' college, weddings, and our retirement, at least those are things we will personally experience and enjoy. When planning for our death, however, we're not around for the implementation. We are powerless *unless* we plan ahead.

This chapter is separate from the chapter where we discussed life insurance for a reason. Life insurance is used to complete your financial plan for your spouse if you die first, so it's kind of an extension of your financial plan. This chapter is different in that we will focus on planning points that are specific to dying, death, and what has to happen and be dealt with when it occurs. I saved it for last because it's the last thing anybody wants to think about, including me. But, if we think about it and take action, we can ensure that things go as smoothly as possible. Are you ready?

GET ORGANIZED

My dad was one of the smartest people I have ever known. He knew something about everything and a lot about most things. He was constantly reading, thinking, and tinkering. The fact that he didn't have a plan in place wasn't because he didn't know any better. He knew the ins and outs of a lot of it. He just didn't think he was going to die at the young age of 49, so everything turned into a big mess when he did.

Speaking of messes, my dad was notoriously messy. His cluttered office and desk at the newspaper plant were legendary. Piles and piles of paper were stacked on every square inch of table surface, sometimes reaching an unstable height of four feet or so before tumbling down in a domino-like landslide. Somebody had to go through all of that stuff when he died, and that somebody was me. It was nearly impossible to find and identify what was important and relevant to the situation and what was not. For one thing, I was only 22 years old, and for another, it wasn't my stuff.

So, what did I do? I created a three-ring binder and labeled it "Important Stuff," and as I came upon things that we needed, I put them in the three-ring binder. When my two-week leave was up, and as Shelly and I (and Jessica the dog) headed out to the East Coast, I handed the three-ring binder over to my mom.

A three-ring binder is the Navy's answer to just about anything that needs to be organized. I had learned this already in my short time within the ranks. And now, even in the paperless, electronic age we live in today, I still use three-ring binders. Every client of ours gets a three-ring binder divided into sections that provides a quick snapshot of everything that is financially important. More than one client has said to me that their three-ring binder is their most important earthly possession. I know that may sound crazy, but if you have ever experienced the loss of a loved one and had to scrounge around for missing information, you probably understand.

About eight years ago, I briefly did away with three-ring binders for clients. I thought an electronic vault would be better. I was wrong. We keep backups of all of the information in our binders in a vault on the web, but the real physical presence in cardboard, leather, and paper is too important. I encourage you to have a binder for yourself that includes some of the information as shown in the illustration that follows. Don't lock it in a safe deposit box or a safe. Your binder should be somewhere secure in your home, but readily findable and accessible in the case of your death. Every once in a while, update your binder. If I had come across something like this when going through my dad's office, I think things would have worked out a lot better.

Date

Client Name

Estate Information

Location of signed will   _____

Date of last signed will   _____

Executors   _____

     _____

Bank Accounts

Acct#   _____

Title   _____

Transfer on Death? _____

Investment Accounts

Acct#   _____

Title   _____

Transfer on Death? _____

Retirement Accounts

Acct# _____

Custodian _____

Beneficiary _____

Contingent Beneficiary _____

Contingent Beneficiary _____

Acct# _____

Custodian _____

Beneficiary _____

Contingent Beneficiary _____

Contingent Beneficiary _____

Life Insurance

Policy#   Insurance Company
Insured: _____
Coverage Amount: _____
Premium: _____

Riders: _____
Death Benefit: _____

Type of Coverage: _____

Long Term Care

Policy#   Insurance Company
Insured: _____
Coverage Amount: _____
Premium: _____

Rider: _____
Maximum Benefit: _____

Waiting Period: _____

Will

Of course, everybody should have a will. If you don't have one, the state has one for you, but you're probably not going to like it. If you die without a will, it's called intestate succession, and if you have any assets or property at all this is going to create an expensive nightmare for your family. So, you should definitely have a will.

Don't be cheap here. Wills are legal documents that should be prepared by an attorney. It's tempting to just try to find a template online and do it yourself, but this could create problems for your heirs. Wills fall under state laws and statutes which vary from state to state. If you have property in multiple states, or countries for that matter, your attorney will have to address this in your documents.

Your will mainly applies to property and assets that you have formal title or rights to. Your will usually does not list property or assets specifically. This way, it does not have to get updated every time you buy a new truck, for instance. Some states, like Texas, recognize community property. This means you and your spouse probably own a lot of stuff together, half and half, whether you like it or not.

For example, if you have an investment account with a million dollars in it and you die, half of it will probably go into your estate and be directed by your will. The other half is considered your spouse's money, regardless of what your wishes may be. This can lead to some complicated, unintended consequences, so it's important to identify what assets are community property and what assets, if any, are considered separate property.

Many times, the estate attorney will use trusts to accomplish different goals regarding the transfer of your property to your heirs. They will either use inter vivos trusts or testamentary trusts. What's the difference? Inter vivos means that the trust is created while you are still alive, while a testamentary trust springs to life once you are dead. Both kinds of trusts are really handy as they allow you to transfer your assets with specific instructions, guidance, and supervision. Trusts are also used to minimize the impact of estate and gift taxes on large estates and provide liability protection if and when applicable.

A great example of the effective use of a testamentary trust is to designate somebody to take care of your assets in case you and your spouse die and leave minor children behind. If this occurs, a trust is created by the will, a trustee is named, as specified in the will, and the money is taken care of for the benefit of the children until they reach a specified age. At the age specified, the kids then take control of the assets, either within the trust or after the assets are transferred into their names and the trust is dissolved. If you have minor kids, you should definitely consider something like this.

MARITAL AGREEMENTS

Ah, the dreaded prenup. I like to call it a marital agreement because, technically, you can create one anytime you want, either before or after you get married. We all recognize this as a controversial document. If you believe everything you read in *People* magazine, then you know that marital agreements are used by rich, mean, powerful families to screw over a potential unmoneyed beau or belle. They can be, but most of the time, they are used as an effective tool for the benefit of both spouses and their families.

In the case of a second marriage where there are kids from previous marriages involved, we nearly always recommend clients consider a marital agreement. That's because it's an agreement between both spouses, and you can't get that in a will. A will can be written and revised unilaterally by either spouse whereas the marital agreement stands until or unless both spouses revise it together, and the provisions survive through your death. It keeps everybody honest.

For example, Jimmy and Suzie get married. Jimmy has an adult daughter from a previous marriage, and then they have another child together. When Jimmy and Suzie made their wills, they both decided that the proceeds from the sale of the house Jimmy inherited from his mom should go to his oldest child and that everything else should be split between both children equally, 50/50 in their estate plan after both of them are gone. Years later, Jimmy dies.

At the funeral, emotions run high. Harsh words are exchanged, and next thing you know, Suzie and Jimmy's oldest daughter are no longer speaking to each other. Since Suzie is still alive, all of Jimmy's assets become hers. Suzie then decides to update her will and cut Jimmy's daughter out. This happens all of the time. It can be solved a few ways, but the easiest way is to try and specify who owns what assets. If they both had agreed the proceeds from Jimmy's mom's house was Jimmy's separate property, then he could specify its disposition easier and hold Suzie to it.

BUSINESS CONTINUATION PLANS, OR BUY-SELL AGREEMENTS

In the case of my dad's death, as I mentioned, he owned stock in the family newspaper with my grandad, who was 79 at the time. My grandad hadn't been active in the business for many years, and my dad was running it. So, when my dad died, nobody was left to run it, which put the entire plant in jeopardy of going out of business. Since Dad was gone, his salary stopped too, which put a great deal of financial pressure on my mom. The status quo was unsustainable, so within a short time, the newspaper was sold to an outside party. That's called a fire sale. If you want to get a decent price for a business, or anything else, it helps if you aren't in such a hurry.

The moral of the story is that, if you own a business, you need a business continuation plan. A business continuation plan is usually in the form of a shareholder agreement, where everything is laid out regarding what happens in case an owner dies. Usually, the plan calls for one or the other owners to buy out the family of the deceased owner for a specified price or one based upon a formula.

The best plans are insured with life insurance held on the owners that creates liquidity at death, so the transaction can occur. This way, everybody gets what they need. The surviving owner or owners are able to maintain and consolidate control and ownership while the surviving family receives money for their stock at a fair price that allows them to carry on financially.

Power of Attorney

Usually, an estate attorney will draft powers of attorney for you and your spouse, along with some other important documents that relate to healthcare choices. Power of attorney gives someone else the authority to conduct financial transactions on your behalf. If it's a durable power of attorney, that means that the granted powers remain in effect even if you are incapacitated. In all cases, power of attorney terminates upon your death.

This document comes in handy if, for instance, you are mentally or physically unable to take care of financial matters. With power of attorney, your spouse or designated person, can conduct bank or financial transactions as if they were you. So, for instance, if you are in cognitive decline, your family does not have to go through the horrible and dehumanizing process of having you legally designated as incapacitated. They can simply take over financially where you left off. Along those lines, most advisors and planners these days have a trusted contact protocol. You can sign a document with your advisor that authorizes them to communicate with a family member to keep you safe if they believe you are having cognitive issues.

Beneficiaries

On many investment accounts and financial instruments, beneficiary designations are used to specify what happens to your accounts or money when you die. IRAs, 401(k)s, life insurance policies, and most other retirement assets have beneficiary designation forms that you fill out and sign. It's important to pay attention to

147

these and make sure they are always up to date.

Believe it or not, when you designate a beneficiary, your assets completely skip over your will and any careful planning you may have done and go directly to who you put on the form. If that's an ex-spouse, you may have created a problem. The estate attorney who completes your will should also provide instructions on how they want beneficiary designations to be completed. Make sure you take that extra step after signing your will and get all of your beneficiary forms filled out and signed too. As noted, all of your beneficiary designations should be documented in your three-ring binder.

TITLING

Non-retirement assets, like general securities accounts and bank accounts, have special titling that determines how the assets will be treated and transferred when you die. Just like beneficiary designations, you must be careful and ensure account titling dovetails with the intentions of your estate planning as a whole. An account in your name will be considered part of your estate when you die. This means your will takes over and provides instructions to your executor, the person you designated to probate your will, as to what to do with the account. Keep in mind, it can take time for the process of probating your estate to get going. In the meantime, accounts held directly in your name will be restricted.

This restriction means that your spouse or heirs may not be able to access funds for paying for your funeral and important stuff like that until a few weeks have gone by and the will is probated. To avoid this, you can add either a TOD or POD title to your account and specify who gets this money. These stand for transfer on death and payable on death, respectively. The account will still be locked down until a death certificate is available, but with a death certificate, the person you designated as TOD or POD will be able to take control of the funds independent of all the legal stuff going on pertaining to your estate.

This can be good or bad, depending on how the estate shakes out. Once the money in an account transfers TOD or POD, it's completely out of the control of your executor and cannot be recaptured. So, for example, let's say that your estate is valued at $1 million and that your will says you want it divided equally between your two children. If you have an account with $700,000 of investments that transfers TOD to one child, that only leaves $300,000 for the other one.

Besides individual accounts with TOD and POD designations, you can have joint accounts. Most of us have joint accounts with our spouse that allow both spouses full authority on the accounts for writing checks, investing, and so forth. Joint accounts are usually either designated as joint tenants with rights of survivorship (JTWROS) or tenants in common (TIC). Property, like your home, is usually also held jointly in a similar fashion. If your joint account with your spouse is JTWROS, then when you die, this account solely becomes your spouse's account. This is great, unless your estate planning calls for something different. Many times, especially with large investment accounts and multiple heirs, a TIC title works better. TIC splits the joint account in half, with one half going to the surviving owner and the other half into the estate so that it can be split among the heirs based upon your will.

TRUSTS

A few of our clients end up with a trust in lieu of a will. Sometimes it's called a living trust. When done properly, a living trust avoids probate so that, when you die, the trust provisions dictate what happens to your stuff instead of a will. It's not as common in Texas as it is in other states because probate is fairly inexpensive here. But in other states, a living trust can save a lot of money in court costs, taxes, and attorney fees.

For some people, the privacy of a living trust is appealing. Probate is a public process, so, when you die, your will is recorded as a public document along with any proceedings. A living trust is a private document that nobody sees unless you show it to them. The trick or challenge with living trusts is to try to get all of your assets into the trust. If you miss anything, then your estate will have to go through probate anyway.

LETTER TO HEIRS

Not everything about smoothly transitioning your affairs after your death is financial. Where some of the real drama and stress occurs after someone dies is around family heirlooms and important decisions and information that are not dealt with in the will or any other official legal or financial documents. So, after all of the legal documents and estate documents are complete, beneficiary designations changed, and accounts and trusts squared away, something might still be missing. Nowhere in any of the formal planning is there an opportunity to personally address those you leave behind and help them with the daunting task of planning a funeral and wrapping up your affairs.

I always suggest that my clients write a letter to their heirs. It's a hard letter to write. It has to be updated from time to time, and it is tough to know where to start or what to say. Try to do it anyway. Here are some general instructions and guidelines to help you get started. I pulled my letter out of the safe today and used it as a guide for the following bullet points:

- Address your letter to your heirs and explain the letter as general instructions that are not intended to be legally binding.

- Explain where you want to be buried, what pre-planning is in place, and other specific guidance regarding cremation, etc.

- List your favorite music for the service, Bible verses, and suggested participants.

- List out old friends you wish to be notified of your death.

- Name your suggestions for pallbearers.

- Provide guidance for obituary and other records. It is most helpful to be specific with dates, the spelling of names of relatives, work history, residence history, organizations, hobbies, etc. Realize that nobody knows any of this information off the top of their head like you, so save your heirs the time, effort, and stress.

- List your favorite charities.

- Provide general guidance on business issues like buy-sell agreements, client notifications, etc.

- Give general information on life insurance.

- Provide names of key advisors and friends whom you want your heirs to consult with in regard to business and personal financial affairs.

- Finally, provide some comforting words of encouragement, Bible verses, or philosophical insight that you believe will be helpful and remembered.

Like I said, this is a hard letter to write. If you have ever been involved with the planning of a funeral, I am sure you realize how helpful a letter like this can be. Block out time on your calendar and try to knock it out. You can seal it in an envelope and place it in your three-ring binder so that it's handy and readily available to your family in case of your death.

IN CONCLUSION

I was just about to write this final section to try to wrap up what I had written in the previous ten chapters. But it was a Monday morning, and there were a few calls I needed to make first. One of those calls was to a lady who had reached out to me over the weekend. Her sister-in-law is a good client and had made the referral. When I called, she picked up on the first ring. Her mom had passed very recently, and she expected to inherit a modest sum of money. She had no idea what to do and was having a lot of anxiety about how to proceed. Well-intentioned family members had been peppering her with advice and suggestions to the point that she was frozen in indecision and confusion.

As we talked, I discovered she is a retired teacher. Divorced, she lives alone in a nice apartment and gets by fairly well on a modest teacher's pension. She has a little bit of savings, a small amount of credit card debt, and a late model car she leases. Her health is excellent. She loves to travel and is able to find money in her budget to do so.

Her primary concerns revolved around her car, the small amount of credit card debt, and housing. One of her relatives had suggested that she buy a home. "You need to start building equity," he had said to her, regarding the purchase of a home. This is, of course, something we hear all the time, and it can generally be considered good advice. But was this good advice for her situation?

No, it was not. Although she is comfortable currently, ten years from now I suspect her budget will be much tighter as the cost of living outpaces her pension income. Her pension will not keep up with inflation, not to mention the potential expense of a future emergency, medical issue, or long-term care. If she sinks all of her money into a house it will not be readily available for these likely potential future costs.

At her investment level, a home purchase would include a mortgage, probable renovation costs, and of course ongoing maintenance costs that she does not currently have to bear for her rented apartment. I suspect these irregular and ongoing costs could easily consume any extra money she might have, thus limiting her opportunities to travel.

Finally, to be blunt, at 70 years old the "start to build equity" ship has sailed. She would not be building equity for herself, only for her heirs. Clearly, the best course of action was for her to save as much of the inheritance as she can for needs that will most certainly present themselves down the line. I suggested she should pay off the credit card balance due to the high interest rate she was being charged and save the rest.

After explaining my suggestions to her, I could hear the tension and anxiety depart in the tone of her voice. She had not considered purchasing a home previous to it being mentioned and was happy and content with her current situation. She had also not considered the impending costs likely coming her way in the next several years or the important role this money could play in assuaging those costs. Well-intentioned, bad financial advice can really screw up somebody's life. In many instances, like in this case, the advice seems reasonable, but it just doesn't fit the scenario.

We hung up the phone, and I started getting myself ready to write again but decided to take one quick look at my email, a classic procrastination move. One email caught my eye from another client's daughter. She and her husband just had their first baby last year and were looking at purchasing life insurance. They were having a second meeting with a life insurance agent that afternoon, and she was asking for advice on what they should purchase. Both work and provide important income for the family. They just bought a nice home with an impressive mortgage, and now they felt it was important to purchase a sizeable amount of life insurance to protect each other and their growing family.

I applauded their decision and maturity while also taking a brief walk down memory lane, remembering a similar conversation with her parents so many years ago. She and her husband had decided they would purchase large 20-year term policies on each other. At their young age it was very inexpensive and fit well into their budget. I approved. But the agent was really pushing hard for them to also purchase a whole life policy on their baby. The premium was modest yet relevant, and they were having a hard time understanding the complexities of the illustrations, guarantees, riders, and advice their agent was providing to them. I explained to her the benefits of the policy, how it would provide guaranteed coverage for the life of their child and even possibly some opportunities for her to increase the coverage later without having to prove insurability. This meant that if their baby was diagnosed with diabetes, cancer, or any other health conditions, she would still have this coverage.

But I also explained that the coverage they were purchasing on each other was much more important than the coverage on their daughter. The agent was strongly touting the cash value buildup of the policy and how this money could be used for their child's college, wedding, a first home purchase, etc. I explained to her that, although her agent's claims were true, there were much better and more efficient ways to save for these goals. It would be unwise to purchase this policy based solely upon the cash accumulation. She thanked me for my thoughts and later let me know they had passed on the whole life coverage for their baby. They felt it was more beneficial to take that money and save it monthly in an investment account for future college expenses. I think they will be glad they did.

Advice from financial salespeople can sound really good, but many times it benefits the salesperson and their company more than it benefits you. Unfortunately, you may not realize it until many years down the road, when the product you were sold doesn't quite deliver as promised. I recently worked with another couple where a poor decision to purchase life insurance as an investment completely destroyed their retirement savings. Don't let this happen to you.

Not long after finishing up this string of emails, an old friend and client dropped by. I knew why he's there. He's going to fire me. In recent years we had not been in alignment. Like so many Americans, his worldview and politics had drifted into extreme territory. That's okay. I have friends and clients across the entire political spectrum. His error, however, was that he had started to confuse his political views with his investment plan.

I remember back in 2012 how many conservatives took extreme measures with their money when Obama was re-elected President. In 2016 it was just the opposite. As liberals predicted Trump would drive the country into the ground, they made emotional investment decisions based upon *their* beliefs. In both cases, they missed out on incredible market growth that's impossible to capture when you are not invested in the stock market.

There is a local advisor on the radio here who hangs his hat on the assurance to his listeners that he can foresee market downturns and get you out safely before you lose any significant money. He uses market indicators as a catalyst for his magic crystal ball. When current market valuations cross or dip below the average, it triggers a sale of all positions into cash. There is more to it, but it's not important for you to fully understand because it doesn't work. As we have discussed previously, the stock market is a million times more complicated than that.

Anyway, this advisor touts his magic to listeners on Saturday afternoons, many of whom are primed and ready to believe what he has to say. By the time Saturday rolls around, most of them have already voluntarily bombarded themselves with the sensational entertainment some call news from their favorite political pundits, Facebook posts, and television networks. It's easy to get worked up in an angry and fearful frenzy if you consume too much of this stuff. This advisor's message is keenly targeted for people in this dangerous frame of mind. I say dangerous because investment decisions made from an emotional state are rarely good decisions.

This is, unfortunately, where my client's current frame of mind resides. I wished my friend the best of luck as he headed down this path. There is not much I can do about it. Everybody gets to make their own decisions about these things, but my advice is to stay clear of any advisor who assures you that they can see the future. Also, along those lines, try to limit your exposure to sensational news and angry political debate; it's not good for your mental health *or* your pocketbook.

There's a lot of information out there, too much, really. And while there is so much information, and maybe because of it, there is very little understanding. That's why I wrote this book. I didn't write it to provide you with everything you need to know. Rather, I wrote it to hopefully provide you with everything you need to *understand.* Now that you understand the basic concepts behind planning, investing, insurance, and the many other puzzle pieces we discussed, you can easily figure out what you need to know. Anybody can go open a Roth IRA because they read somewhere that it's a good idea, but then what? The next thing they read maybe says that they should pay off their home mortgage, so the Roth goes by the wayside. Only when you conceptually understand the important concepts and building blocks that we discussed in this book can you then effectively use tools, like Roth IRAs, to achieve your long-term goals.

There's a lot of advice out there too. As we discussed, it's hard, if not impossible, for consumers to distinguish the good from the bad or the conflicted from the unbiased. Armed with the knowledge and understanding you gained from Chapter 5, you'll have to wade through the advice you receive and make your own determinations. Your safest and easiest course of action is to find a fee-only advisor, like myself, and pay them to keep your plan on the straight and narrow.

My door is open to you. If you have questions or need further assistance, all you have to do is reach out to me at rob.schulz@schulzwealth.com, and I'll do my best to help in any way I can. I also moderate a group on Facebook where members support one another in our efforts to achieve financial success in face of life's numerous obstacles. Just search for the group "Thoughts on Things Financial" on Facebook or follow the URL https://www.facebook.com/groups/thoughtsonthingsfinancial/ and ask for permission to join.

It looks like I was able finish my conclusion despite all the interruptions. This book has been an enjoyable journey for me. It has provided a way for me to say to a broader audience some things that I say regularly in client meetings. I hope you enjoyed the journey as well.

Fair winds,

Rob

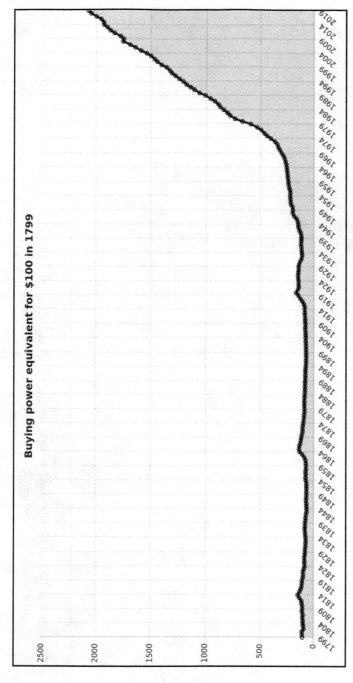

This image from Chapter 2 can be found online at: https://www.investopedia.com/ask/answers/042415/what-impact-does-inflation-have-time-value-money.asp: "What Impact Does Inflation Have on the Dollar Value Today?"

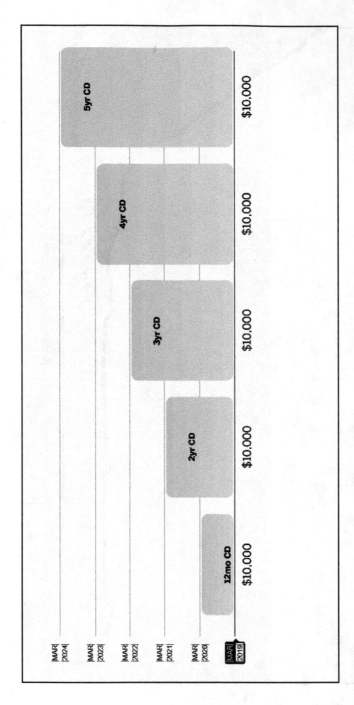

This image from Chapter 4 can be found online at: https://www.ally.com/do-it-right/banking/cd-laddering-how-to-build-a-cd-ladder/, "Give Your Returns a Boost: How to Build a CD Ladder With the Ally Bank CD Ladder Tool"

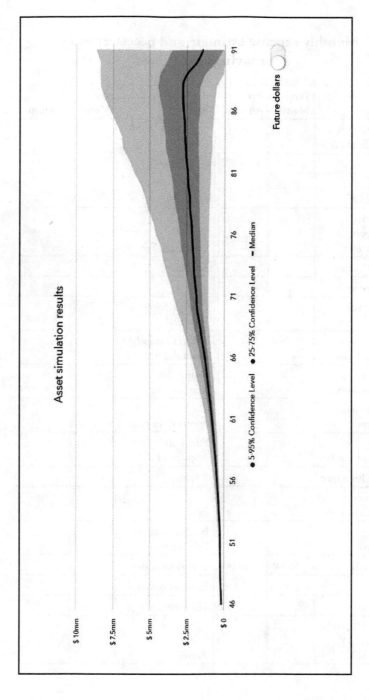

Asset simulation results

Future dollars

● 5-95% Confidence Level   ● 25-75% Confidence Level   — Median

$ 10mm

$ 7.5mm

$ 5mm

$ 2.5mm

$ 0

46   51   56   61   66   71   76   81   86   91

Monthly expense estimate and necessary range for savings worksheet

Item	Per Month	Per Annum	Item	Per Month	Per Annum
LOANS & LIABILITIES			OTHER LIVING COSTS		
Mortgage			Childcare		
2nd or HELOC			Clothing		
Home/ Property Insurance			School/ University Fees		
HOA Dues			Allowance		
Property Tax					
Personal Loans			Clothes/Shoes - Personal		
Auto Lease			Entertainment/ Restaurants		
Auto Loan			Gym/Club Membership		
Investment Loans			Sports & Fitness		
Credit Cards			Furniture/ Appliances		
Life Insurance			Books		
Income Protection			Pet Costs		
Other			Netflix/Amazon Subscriptions		
TOTAL:	$0.00	$0.00	Gifts/Donations		
			Lunch/Coffee		
			Holidays		
HOME, UTILITY, HEALTH			Travel		

Rent			Other		
Water			**TOTAL:**	$0.00	$0.00
Electricity					
Gas					
Cable/SAT TV			TRANSPORTATION		
Home Phone			Car Insurance		
Mobile Phone			Car Fuel		
Internet			Car Repairs & Maintenance		
Home Maintenance			Transport Costs (Bus, etc.)		
Household Help			Other		
Yard Maintenance			**TOTAL:**	$0.00	$0.00
Groceries					
Medical/ Dental Consultations					
Private Health Insurance					
Pharmacy/ Prescriptions			Accountant		
Other			Attorney		
TOTAL:	$0.00	$0.00			

Life insurance needs analysis worksheet

LIFE INSURANCE NEEDS ANALYSIS					
			John	Molly	
Liquid Assets					
	Cash/Checking		$30,000	$30,000	
	Savings		$14,000	$14,000	
	Bonds				
	Life Insurance		$123,000	$157,000	
	Term at Work			$120,000	
		TOTAL	$137,000	$291,000	
Liabilities (to be paid off if client dies today)					
	Mortgage (only if house is to be sold)		$0	$0	
	Debts		$0	$0	
	Final Medical Expenses		$17,500	$17,500	
	Funeral Expenses		$8,000	$8,000	
	Probate		$1,500	$1,500	
	Estate Taxes		$0	$0	
	Adjustment Fund		$9,800	$58,800	
		TOTAL	$36,800	$85,800	
	TOTAL IMMEDIATE NEED		-$100,200	-$205,200	

PV of Income Needed with Children			$0	$210,966
Education			$120,000	$120,000
PV of Income Need during Blackout			$0	$290,325
PV of Income Need in Retirement			$0	$0
Emergency Fund				
	TOTAL FINANCIAL NEED		$120,000	$621,291
	TOTAL LIFE INSURANCE NEED		$19,800	$416,091

CPSIA information can be obtained
at www.ICGtesting.com
Printed in the USA
LVHW021242040920
665076LV00016B/743